Manifesting Love

Real Life Love Stories of Conscious Relationships Co-created with the Universe

**Created and Compiled
by Andrea Pennington, MD, C.Ac.**

Featuring stories by:
Karan Joy Almond & Eric Gerson
Abbey Kelly — Lene Nielsen
Ofkje Teekens — Margaretha Tosi
Karena Virginia — Lee-Anne Wine

Foreword by Michael Bernard Beckwith

MAKE YOUR MARK GLOBAL

Manifesting Love © 2020 Andrea Pennington, MD, C. Ac., Karan Almond, Eric Gerson, Abbey Kelly, Lene Nielsen, Ofkje Teekens, Margaretha Tosi, Karena Virginia, Lee-Anne Wine

Published by Make Your Mark Global Publishing, LTD

The purpose of this book is not to give medical advice, nor to give a prescription for the use of any technique as a form of treatment for any physical, medical, psychological, or emotional condition. The information in this book does not replace the advice of a physician, either directly or indirectly. It is intended only as general information and education. In the event that you use any of the information in this book for yourself, as is your constitutional right, the authors and publisher assume no responsibility for your actions. No expressed or implied guarantee of the effect of the use of any of the recommendations can be given. The authors and publisher are not liable or responsible for any loss or damage allegedly arising from any information in this book. Many of the names and personal details have been changed to protect the privacy of individuals.

Without limiting the rights under copyright reserved above, no part of this publication may be reproduced, stored in, or introduced into a retrieval system, or transmitted in any form or by any means (electronic, mechanical, photocopying, recording, or otherwise), without the prior written permission of the copyright owners.

The scanning, uploading, and distribution of this book via the Internet or any other means without the permission of the publisher are illegal and punishable by law. Please purchase only authorized electronic editions and do not participate in or encourage any electronic piracy of copyrightable materials. Your support of the authors' rights is appreciated. *And karma will get you if you violate this anyway!*

While the authors and publisher have made every effort to provide accurate information regarding references and Internet addresses at the time of publication, the authors and publisher do not assume responsibility for errors or changes that occur after publication. The authors and publishers also do not assume any responsibility for third-party websites and/or their content.

Book cover design: Andrea Danon & Stefan Komljenović of Art Biro Network www.artbiro.ba

Back cover painting by Laura Casini

Library of Congress Cataloging-in-Publication Data

Library of Congress Control Number: 2020948934

Manifesting Love: Real Life Love Stories of Conscious Relationships Co-created with the Universe

Publisher: Make Your Mark Global, LTD

Las Vegas, Nevada

Pages - 128

Trade Paperback ISBN 978-1-7356790-1-3

Hardcover ISBN 978-1-7356790-2-0

Ebook ISBN 978-1-7356790-3-7

Subjects: Psychology

Summary: In *Manifesting Love* Dr. Andrea Pennington presents real life love stories of people from various backgrounds and cultures who have dug deep within themselves to find self-love, heal from past trauma, and define what they really want in a romantic relationship. Some have created elaborate rituals and ceremonies to ask the Universe to unite them with their ideal partner. Some have totally surrendered to the process, opening their heart to true love. While another has used the powerful art of Feng Shui to make her home inviting and inspiring for a new partner. What these stories have in common is how they illustrate common strategies and techniques for manifesting a soul-aligned relationship no matter our age or stage of life. There is great hope and inspiration to be found here.

MAKE YOUR MARK GLOBAL PUBLISHING, LTD
USA

Manifesting Love © 2020 *Andrea Pennington*

For information on bulk purchase orders of this book or to book Dr. Andrea to speak at your event or on your program, call +33 06 12 74 77 09 or send an email to Booking@AndreaPennington.com

Also Compiled or Co-authored by Andrea Pennington

The Top 10 Traits of Highly Resilient People

Magic and Miracles

Life After Trauma

Time to Rise

Turning Points / Vendepunkter

Heart to Heart: The Path to Wellness

Resilience Through Yoga and Meditation

Dedication

This book is lovingly dedicated to the beautiful souls
who are praying for, waiting for, and
hoping to find true love

May this book guide you on
your journey to finding the love for yourself within you

And may you be blessed with the deep soul connection to a loving
partner for a fulfilling, conscious relationship

Contents

Preface 1

Foreword 3

Introduction 5

Chapter 1: Your Relationship History 17

    The Love I Wanted Was Always in Me By Abbey Kelly 19

Chapter 2: Your Attachment Style 31

Chapter 3: Uncover The Blocks to Giving and Receiving Love ...43

    Unhealed Wounds 44

    Unspoken Expectations 47

    Mismatched Attachment Styles 48

Chapter 4: Essential Elements for Manifesting 51

    Vision & Intention 52

        Accidentally on Purpose By Karan Joy Almond & Eric Gerson ...56

    Space 65

        Making Room for Love Again By Lene Nielsen 67

    Time 76

        On Manifesting Self-Love By Lee-Anne Wine 77

    Surrender in Faith 85

        This Love Story Was Meant to Be By Ofkje Teekens 86

        I Knew I Loved You Before I Met You By Karena Virginia 95

Chapter 5: Create Your Own Manifesting Process 105

    Manifesting the Love of My Life at 35 By Margaretha Tosi 107

Conclusion 115

Appendix 117

About the Book's Creator 118

Preface

The book you hold in your hands is a collection of very generous, honest stories from courageous authors. Each of them has opened up their heart to bring you insight into what led them out of pain, confusion and heartbreak into their present lives which are full of true intimacy, joy and fulfilling, conscious relationships. These stories of manifesting love demonstrate that there is someone (even several someones!) out there who are perfectly poised to love you.

Because our authors are from a variety of countries and we are publishing these stories in English, you may notice that the spelling of words is sometimes in British English and sometimes in American English, depending on the author's country of origin. You'll also see that some phrases they use are unknown to you, as they are not always direct translations from their mother tongue.

In light of the fact that many of our authors are not native English speakers, our team of editors has worked hard to make each story clear and full of the impact the author intended. It is our sincere hope that we have done their compelling stories justice and that you will be moved and inspired by them.

If you'd like to hear the authors in their own voice and watch as they provide context and color to how they worked their various processes and rituals to manifest true love, I invite you to visit www.ManifestingLoveBook.com to watch interviews conducted by the book's publisher, Dr. Andrea Pennington.

Foreword

Relationships are a core function of living. How we relate to others—from our families, friends, and intimate partners, to our colleagues and the world around us—not only affects *and* is affected by how we see and create our experience of life, it is ultimately a reflection of our primary relationship; that is, the one that we have with ourselves. Simply put, how we relate to and love ourselves determines how we relate to and love others. Now critical to that awareness is the realization that as the divine, eternal beings we are, Love is who and what we are. Love is *the* universal guiding principle and cosmic foundation upon which we and all things in Life exist. Understanding this truth is key to understanding the nature of Life itself.

In my series of essays, *Eight Principles For Thriving Relationships*, I write that, "Many people desire to enter relationships without understanding the essential nature of who they are to begin with. Before we can talk about the relationship with another, there has to be discussion around the relationship with one's own Self, as well as the proper context for that relationship." Moreover, just as with any other aspect of our lives, the purpose of relationship cannot be separated from our purpose for being here on the planet, which is to reveal, express, and expand humanity's capacity for Love.

See, the love that we yearn for and think we seek from others, is actually the inner urgings of our soul's desire to express itself as the Love we are, and to create our relationships and lives accordingly. In fact, Self-love is our one and only True Love, and it is this awareness that allows us to radiate that Love to everyone and everything around us. Cultivating authentic Self-Love is the engine that powers our ability to create more joy, more peace, more harmony, and more abundance in our lives. It is the mental, emotional, and spiritual juice that strengthens and vitalizes us and our relationships.

And it is a remarkable practice, process, and adventure on which Dr. Pennington's book will take you!

Manifesting Love is a beautiful manifesto on the art, science, and the generating power of authentic Self-love. It leads readers on a deeply intentional, empowering, healing, and revealing inward odyssey, and provides opportunities for insights and revelations on remembering, recognizing, drawing out, and radiating Love. Practicing authentic Self-love opens the doorway to the discovery and conscious realization that Love is omnipresent, and that it only seeks to amplify, multiply, and expand itself through and as our lives and relationships. In-joy the journey.

Peace & Richest Blessings,
Michael Bernard Beckwith
Founder & Spiritual Director, Agape International Spiritual Center
Author, Life Visioning, Spiritual Liberation, and TranscenDance Expanded

Introduction

Your desire to manifest love is an essential first step toward enjoying a healthy relationship. In addition to desire, you need to believe that it's possible for you. Do you believe that there is a loving partner for you to enjoy a fulfilling relationship in this lifetime? I do.

Somewhere on this planet, there is a beloved man or woman who is perfect for you. I believe that there is a beautiful soul who will accept you, love you and cherish you for many years to come. If you've given up hope about finding love, I invite you to put pessimism aside and consider that with nearly 8 billion people on Earth, there is certainly someone (or several someones!) with whom you can have a healthy and loving relationship. This book will inspire you to believe in the upcoming reality of being united with your beloved.

If you've spent years feeling lonely and sad, wishing that your ideal partner would drop from the sky to put your isolation to an abrupt end, I invite you to take a more active role in attracting your partner. This book will provide you with a process of preparing for and calling forth that loving relationship using a process known as manifestation.

If you have worried that you are too broken, too damaged, too old or not 'enough' to attract a partner, then you will find that this book will help you see yourself in a healthier light. Even if you have old heartbreak or a history of abandonment or betrayal, you can heal the parts of you that were wounded and embrace your authentic self with compassion and self-love. And you can be joined with a partner who loves you for exactly who you are now.

This is another essential ingredient you need to believe before you manifest a life partner — and that is, even with wound or scars, you are worthy of love. You don't need a rescuer or savior, and certainly not someone to make you 'whole'. You are already whole, even if you are wounded. And you are lovable, even if you've made mistakes.

It's natural to seek love

We are all born with a deep desire to be accepted, to belong, and to feel cherished. Hardwired into our nervous system is the impulse to seek out close connections, first for safety, then for companionship, and ultimately for mutual growth and support. And so the drive to search for intimate love relationships is an inescapable part of life. It isn't a blemish to your character to desire love. It's one of the essential human needs.

For many of us, however, there are nuances beneath this basic desire that influence our choice in partners. Unconscious drivers, which we often do not fully understand, lie hidden among the innate impulses and needs, which impact our success in maintaining a relationship. For example, how often do we stop to investigate why we are attracted to some people and not others? Have you ever asked what kind of person would be best suited for you? How aware are you of our own assumptions, preferences and programming and how they affect your behavior in romantic love? These questions, and many more, have driven my personal curiosity on the subject of romantic love for decades.

My self-inquiry at the age of 24 began with trying to understand why I felt so compelled to get married. Halfway through medical school, I felt that I was too young and not ready at all for marriage. Yet seeing a handful of fellow medical students coupling and marrying initiated the desire in me — or so I thought. I now understand that the impulse to couple is a biological drive that is socially propagated and has been influencing our relationship goals for over a century.

While discussing this revelation over dinner during a girls' night out, a classmate of mine asked me what type of guy I liked. Slightly

Introduction

confused, I admitted that I didn't know if I had a type. I replied that I just liked handsome guys, and that I needed to feel some sort of spark or connection with them. I added that it didn't matter if they were white or black, in professional roles or not.

In my early thirties this same friend gave me a book that dramatically accelerated my personal investigation of love and provided a deeper understanding that has forever changed my life. *Getting the Love You Want* by Harville Hendrix and his wife, Helen LaKelly Hunt, introduced me to the concept of Imago Relationship Therapy. I learned how the early childhood experiences with our parents and caretakers create an ideal image of a mate, what Harville and Helen call the imago. An amalgamation of the positive and negative qualities of our caretakers, the imago is part of what drives our search for and attraction to certain romantic partners over others.

I came to understand how my parents' divorce initiated my fragile sense of self worth and insatiable need for validation in many areas of life, especially in romantic relationships. This knowledge opened my eyes to the subconscious attraction I felt for men who appeared strong, my vision of handsome, intelligent, and possessing certain personality traits. It also initiated me on a path of discovering why unconsciously, I both pulled in and repelled men by repeating certain behavior patterns when the relationship took a turn toward deep intimacy. I soon became fascinated with the psychology behind love, attraction and relationship sustainability.

A thorough review of attachment theory and the healing of attachment trauma, including the works of John Bowlby, Mary Ainsworth, Amir Levine, Rachel S. E. Heller, R. Chris Fraley, Laurel Parnell, and Gay and Kathlyn Hendricks helped me to perceive and heal my relationship dynamics in transformative ways. Then, with the addition of neuroscience research around the biochemistry of love, I deepened my understanding of the mating and selection drives of mammals and how millions of years of evolution make human love relationships in the current era particularly challenging.

Over the last two decades I have absorbed all of that psychological research plus the works of Helen Fisher, PhD, Esther Perel, Daniel Amen, MD, Robert Johnson and countless others to unravel the mystery behind my brain chemistry in love, my attachment style, my internal sabotage patterns, and my limiting beliefs to finally discover and embrace unconditional self-acceptance and self-love. I have compiled several self-discovery practices and self-love techniques in my book, *The Real Self Love Handbook*. (For more books on our suggested reading list, please see the *Appendix*).

This knowledge, processing the many relationship experiences I've had, along with my own spiritual evolution has equipped me to open my heart to love and to enjoy deeply fulfilling relationships. I've shared this information with my audiences over the years with a warm reception. Now I'm inspired to share this insight with any and all who are open to it, to bring more love and healing to our world.

Aware, equipped and prepared

My aim with this book, my workshops, the #RealSelfLove Movement and the Conscious Love podcast is to **make the unconscious conscious** as it pertains to self-love and romantic relationships. My mission is to bring your internal drives, wounds, preferences, values, dreams and desires out of the shadows of your subconscious mind and the corners of your heart into your awake, conscious mind so that you can heal, embrace your whole self and thrive in relationships as your Authentic Self. I believe that when you've uncovered who you really are, defined what you truly value in life, and aligned your heart and mind with the goal of living a conscious love story, you are more ready to manifest love.

Introduction

With this book we provide a framework of self-discovery that will lead to increased self-awareness so that you manifest a love story in alignment with who you really are. Some practices and inquiries will enhance your clarity on what you want to experience in relationship. You'll also discover tools and meditations for healing your past wounds, thus making you more equipped for the journey of manifestation. And all of this exploration should help you feel prepared for living authentically and loving wholeheartedly. And where you still need growth, this book and the stories shared here will inspire you to learn more.

Manifesting from neediness or a sense of lack

The myth of romantic love makes us believe that we are not complete and will never be complete unless and until we find our 'other half.' Many couples in longterm, happy relationships say that they feel more complete or whole thanks to their beloved's presence. When pressed to unpack this concept further we find two key distinctions that both happy couples and relationship therapists agree upon:

1) Relationships can provide a safe container for an individual or both parties to heal and thus return to an innate state of wholeness.

2) A healthy relationship can provide an arena for complete self-expression that can make an individual feel wholly alive.

To be clear, it is not my belief that finding a partner will complete you. You are already whole. You may need some of your broken pieces to be mended though. There may be hidden parts of you which need to be brought to the light in a configuration which brings you peace, vitality and self-love. And it may be true that in a healthy relationship you may feel more free to be your whole self.

Why is it important to grasp this distinction? Because the people you find attractive, and those attracted to you will vary based on the energy you radiate. When you assume that you are broken or lacking something, you will naturally search for what you think is missing, often in a needy or desperate way. This is an unconscious mental search that often leads to relationship pairings that are not fulfilling on the deepest level because they are driven by a false sense of lack.

You may attract someone who comes into your life to confirm your doubts, suspicions and assumptions about relationships or your worth. They appear in the role of teacher to show you, often through pain or disappointment, what you need to see and learn to return to Truth. (Truth being the fact that you are perfect and whole, at your core, and you do not need anyone to validate your worthiness of love.)

Another person may show up to fill your supposed deficit but won't end up truly fulfilling you on the levels needed for lasting companionship, intimacy and mutual growth. This often leads to disappointment that can also point the way to the Truth.

When you are connected with your Authentic Self at a heart level, knowing that you are whole, lovable and worthy, you will be attracted to, and you will attract well matched souls, including partners with whom you could have a mutually rewarding, loving relationship. That's why I recommend that you examine your beliefs and check in with your heart to determine from what perspective you are manifesting. This point will be reinforced as you read the stories in this book.

Healing your heart & restoring wholeness

Healing from childhood trauma, past relationship drama, heartbreak or heartache is an essential step for manifesting your longterm partner. But you don't need to be totally healed before manifesting a new relationship. As long as you are emotionally stable, there is nothing wrong with entering a relationship which could provide the basis for self-discovery, mutual healing and soul-aligned growth.

This is a beautiful gift that can come from conscious coupling. For some it is the most effective way to heal from early childhood wounds, abuse or abandonment. If you have any of those in your emotional history it is best to have a conscious understanding and awareness of the impact that your past has on you manifesting process. In Chapter 1 you'll review your own relationship history to examine the influences on your dating choices and identify patterns to be changed and wounds to be healed.

Attachment Styles

The way your primary caregivers attended to your needs as a child created a blueprint for how you experience your needs and how you seek to meet those needs in relationships. Your attachment style dictates whether you feel secure, insecure, avoidant, clingy or dismissive in relationships. In Chapter 2 we will explore how your attachment style impacts your attraction patterns, along with other influences, so that you can be mindful and aware of the conscious choices you make as you embark on your manifesting journey.

Teachers, soulmates & twin flames

I want to provide a note of caution and reemphasize why it is wise to be conscious of how your past programming and relationship experiences have primed you to be attracted to certain people over others. Attracting a partner that triggers a familiar feeling, instant attraction with a strong magnetic pull is often taken as a sign that you are being drawn toward your lifelong partner. However, it may also be the sign that you're meeting your next 'teacher', soulmate or twin flame.

I realize these last two terms may seem a bit new age, but they've become so commonly used that they are worth a bit of definition. While I am not purporting to be an expert on these two concepts, I have learned that soulmate and twin flame relationships may include deep ties to soul contracts and maybe even past life experiences.

Experts on the subject say that a soulmate often brings unfinished business to the relationship, which you two are bound to work through. Often, the instant chemistry and strong attraction may be taken as a sign that you've met 'the one', your true soul mate. And that may be true. While there can be deep love in soul mate relationships, often, there is a deep wound to be healed. And each partner may feel triggered, agitated and irritated until the wounds are healed. The soul mate connection can lead to growth, healing and learning. And since we often learn the most during painful life lessons that come through relationships, the soul mate connection is not totally bad. It's just important to note that relationships with instant, strong chemistry may bring some bad along with the rush of good feelings.

A twin flame is often described as a mirror that brings an entangled love-hate component with the relationship. Some describe the familiar feeling and attraction in a twin flame set up as being a result of you seeing the best of you in them, and vice versa. However, seeing yourself in another can also bring out the worst qualities. Ultimately, there is something that needs to be worked through, possibly even energetic ties to cut so that you can be you, and your partner can be themselves as individuals. You'll read about Karan and Eric in Chapter 4, who believe they are twin flames, and how they manage the fire storm their relationship has brought them. They even share relationship advice on YouTube, because the dynamics of that kind of relationship are so unique!

Another connection that may feel eerily familiar and attractively comfortable is one we find with 'teachers' who are sent to us to help us learn lessons on our soul journey. For example, I have seen clients who grew up in an abusive family go on to have a string of toxic relationships with abusive partners. Many a therapy session has uncovered red flags and warning signs that were ignored because things felt so right, comfortable, easy. For example, I have heard clients express that there was something familiar and attractive about their partner, and the were saddened to see that they turned out to be narcissists with similar abuse patterns to their parents.

Armed with this awareness, if in future encounters, if they notice a potential partner displays certain characteristics or elicits a feeling of comfort quickly, before they really know the person, they take it as a sign to be more aware. This allows time to tease out why and what attracted them, such as familiar speech patterns, scents, and they way they are being treated. This helps some recognize the potential for yet another disappointing relationship, and the choice to end the connection early.

Left to continue, that person could have taken on the role of teacher—not consciously, but figuratively. The lessons learned in a relationship with a teacher may be to recognize your own worth, to set better boundaries, or to change the type of people you date. Again, it's not bad to manifest a teacher, but it may come with pain and disappointment.

Relationship inventory

One way to get a clear idea of how and why your attraction system is primed to certain people and not others is to look over your relationship history. Using the Relationship Inventory worksheet in Chapter 1, you are invited to look back on your past relationships, including the ones with your parents or caretakers, and list the qualities that stand out in your memory, both positive and negative. You will write down how your parents and partners treated you, and how they made you feel. Once you summarize the lessons you learned from past relationships, which may include lessons about yourself, your sense of worthiness, and your willingness to accept and give love, you can see how you may be subconsciously drawn to someone to complete the 'unfinished business' of the past.

If you see any value gained from lessons learned in relationships that included pain, betrayal or disappointment, you can now consider the positive value you took away from those experiences. This can help you put those old issues to rest, embrace forgiveness for yourself or for the other parties involved.

If you find that there any residual resentments, feelings of guilt, shame or low self-worth lingering as a result, I have recorded a guided meditation available for download that will help you reframe your past experiences and release any negative energy or emotion tied to past relationships, including with your parents, family or caretakers. The emotional residue needs to be removed so that you can move forward with a clean emotional slate, an open heart and a clear mind. (The link to download all of the guided meditations and worksheets is in the *Appendix*.)

Becoming a vibrational match for your beloved

We can truly manifest what we most desire and what we most wish for, and the science of physics can influence the process. It is often said that you get what you ask for and receive what you radiate. Therefore, we need to be mindful and aware of what we are asking for — consciously and unconsciously. The Universe can and will respond to our wishes, so our goal with this book is to show you a variety of ways of preparing yourself and your environment for bringing the manifestation to reality.

Before manifesting, we suggest that you get into a brainwave pattern that aligns you with your heart and subconscious mind to get clear on what you really want or need. Being in a higher state of consciousness through brainwave entrainment and meditation can help you see, with discernment, what your true desire is in the present versus what has been conditioned from your past.

To support you in this process, I've included some meditation audios that are designed to put you into a state of heart-aligned harmony. This is important because if you manifest from your busy mind you may manifest a teacher. A teacher will likely bring you more pain until you learn the lesson needed.

When our mind is no longer telling us what to do, we are better able to surrender to the wisdom of the Universe, the wisdom of the heart and soul. When you manifest consciously, from the heart, you get what is best for your soul journey and you can choose to attract experiences that bring joy and ease for your evolution.

The structure of this book

In Chapter 1 you will explore your relationship history to uncover wounds and any unconscious tendencies to choose poorly matched partners you may have. The personal story of Abbey Kelly, a relationship coach for women, shows us how a low sense of self-worth can be a major hindrance to fulfilling relationships. As a result of her own relationship inventory she set herself on a healing path of self-love and now does the same for the women she coaches.

In Chapter 2 you will have a succinct overview of attachment styles to better understand how your past experiences have shaped how you attempt to get your needs met in relationships. This provides excellent insights on how and why you feel the way you do, and what to do to have more peace as you enter your manifesting process.

In Chapter 3 we outline ways to overcome common blocks to manifesting love, including unhealed wounds, unspoken expectations, unconscious patterns, and mismatched attachment styles. I share my own story of how I resolved some of the unhealed wounds of my inner child, which helped me open up to new love. And you'll also get access to a healing meditation which you can download that is helpful if you're still in the healing process.

In Chapter 4 we outline the essential elements needed for preparing for a new relationship including setting your intention and having a clear vision, like the story by Karan Almond and Eric Gerson beautifully illustrates. You'll understand the importance of making time for yourself and your new partner, like Lee-Anne Wine's journey shows us. Plus, creating space for your beloved is explored with the heartfelt story by Lene Nielsen. And you'll see what it takes to surrender with faith to the process, as the stories of Karena Virginia and Ofkje Teekens highlight.

Finally in Chapter 5 you will have a detailed explanation of how to create your own manifesting ceremony. Whether you do it silently in your mind or with a full on ritual, as Margaretha Tosi's story outlines, you will be able to make concrete steps to call forth your new love.

Shall we begin your conscious manifestation process now?

Chapter 1
Your Relationship History

Your Relationship History

We each have an underlying map for how we show up in relationships that guides us to attract certain types of people and not others. Knowing you have this map can point out ways to best experience harmony and deep connection in relationships going forward. This baseline blueprint is mainly an unconscious structure along which you navigate the murky waters of interpersonal connection.

If you've repeatedly attracted emotionally unavailable, narcissistic, or abusive partners it may time to explore whether there is something hidden in the shadows of your subconscious mind that is influencing your choices. Bringing the unconscious drivers of your behaviors, biases and preferences can help you be really clear and intentional with your manifesting process.

By taking a relationship inventory you can also get a clear picture of what you've been settling for, tolerating or forgiving in relationships which is not healthy nor sustainable. This is precisely what helped Abbey Kelly establish clear boundaries and stop settling for guys who didn't hang around after the relationship became physically intimate. Abbey's story highlights the value of looking back over your relationship history to understand the characteristics past partners had that you want to steer clear of as you manifest your next relationship.

The Love I Wanted Was Always in Me

By Abbey Kelly

It's hard to believe there are plenty of fish in the sea if none of them want to be caught. Throughout my twenties, I would date boys, but nothing was ever serious. No one ever wanted to make it official with me. Despite seeming totally interested in the beginning, they disappeared without an explanation, leaving me to wonder what I was doing wrong. I thought we were doing great. He used to text me all the time, why has he stopped? Is there something wrong with me? Am I too independent? Maybe I seem uninterested, perhaps I took too long to respond... I kept on attracting guys who were emotionally unavailable, still attached to their ex, or not ready to commit but always down to fuck.

In my first year at university, I was in a 'situation-ship'. But at that time, with my zero dating experience, I thought we were in a relationship. Silly me, he only wanted one thing from me, and after that, he left me for another girl that he liked more. Ouch, that hurt. Nobody explained to me or my ego the rules of dating or the games that some men play just to get what they want out of you. And it's not always for sex. As I got closer to thirty and looked back over my dating history, I realised that some grown men were using me as a placeholder/therapist just to fill a void in their emotional life. It's funny, because I used to hear men say, "Women hit a wall at thirty." No, dude. Women just tend to wise up, and your BS is no longer valid or even tolerated.

Well, at least not by me.

Backstory

David still hadn't replied to my text, which I had sent sometime in January. Messaging him was my one last attempt at lowering my dignity to remind him that I still existed. Maybe five weeks later, he gave me a casual reply asking me how I was doing. He didn't even acknowledge the previous text that I had sent him. I simply deleted his number.

I had just finished chemotherapy and I wanted to focus on myself. I was feeling like a brand-new woman, and something in me finally clicked in place. I realised that I deserved better. I mean, I was being treated for cancer, and he couldn't even be bothered to check in with me regularly. I told myself going forward that he didn't deserve one more second of my time, energy or thoughts. It was a shame, because I'd had high hopes for us.

A few weeks after me not replying to his text, I got a phone call. (I wasn't really surprised it was him—all these F-boy ghosts love to haunt the living). There was a lot of awkward silence after I basically told him that I wasn't here for his ghosting BS. He agreed with me, and the conversation more or less ended in a civil manner.

Choosing myself

Over the summer I did some solo traveling. I had always wanted to travel to California, but it was something I wanted to do with the love of my life. But whilst I was lying in my hospital bed, I had the realisation that life really is short. I needed to spend more time actually doing the things that I love and enjoy, with or without a man by my side.

Traveling alone helped take my mind off my illness and all the F-boys that were not worthy of my thoughts. When I got back home to London, I was in a much better headspace. I stumbled upon Abraham Hicks on YouTube, and I would listen to her every single day. I was so keen to make positive changes in my life. I just wanted to be happy again.

Whilst I was in London, I briefly got into a relationship with a guy I'd met on Tinder. Sadly, due to his personal issues, I decided to break up with him. I felt that it was for the best. I still needed to work on myself and didn't want to take on his problems. Feeling a little low, I decided to see what David was up to on social media. And just when I thought I couldn't get any lower, I clicked on his page (sit down for this one).

I saw that David was in a long-distance relationship. Even worse, he was engaged. My heart sank. I leaned back in my chair in disbelief. He could do N.Y. to Paris, but he couldn't hop on a two-hour train ride to visit me in London whilst I was sick? What a prick. I felt cheap and used. How could he do that to me? How could I do that to myself?

Deep down, I knew I had chosen to ignore the fact that we were going nowhere. He had made a great first impression, and I had been in awe of what we could be rather than what we were, which was absolutely nothing. He used to message me around nine p.m. to hang out at his place. He wouldn't even offer to pick me up, which goes to show just how much he thought of me and how little I thought of myself.

I started to really question my behaviour. Why was I putting so much energy into guys who were not really my boyfriends, and who were making little effort to impress me? It wasn't even just about David; it was about all the F-boys before him. I had to reflect on my actions. I did a self-analysis to figure out why I was trying so hard to prove myself to men, and I came to the bitter conclusion I was a low-value woman. I had low standards, low self-esteem, and I let boys overstep my boundaries. I was just trying to be the cool girl, the girl who doesn't make a fuss, the girl who didn't hold boys accountable for their actions. It hurt to admit it, but it wasn't them. It was me.

I knew that being in self-pity mode wasn't going to help me. I was tired of not getting the respect I deserved, tired of the ghosting, tired of the breadcrumbing, tired of being the cool girl who was too timid to speak on the red flags. I knew for things to change, I had to change.

How I manifested love

Years ago, my mum gave me a book called *The Secret*, so I was very familiar with the Law of Attraction. I had already used it to manifest other great things in my life, so I thought, why not try to manifest love?

I reached for my diary and began scripting. The new, strong, wiser me who says no and has boundaries is manifesting a new man. I wrote as if I were already the woman that I wanted to become.

I then went on to write about how I wanted to feel in the relationship, how I wanted my partner to feel, and how I wanted to be treated. I wrote about all the things we'll be doing together: travelling, watching the sunset, counting stars in the sky, eating at fancy restaurants, going to the cinema, having real dates. I also told the universe in my written manifestation that I wanted to be attracted to him. After I finished writing, I closed my eyes and got a flash of a man in a tropical place.

Once I had written my manifestation, I didn't want to spend my time obsessing about how or when it would happen. That's the universe's job. My job was to put all my time and energy back into improving me. I told myself going forward that I am a high-value woman who respects herself. I will not be lowering my standards. I don't need to change or fix a man to make him fit into my world. He either does or he doesn't, and that's it.

Reconnecting with my femininity

Growing up, I had been a tomboy. Then, as I approached adulthood, the outside world convinced me that women who wear makeup are insecure or trying to impress men. Now I realised that my divine self wanted me to be more in contact with my femininity. I started to wear makeup on a daily basis, and I loved the way I looked. During the spring and summer, I wore more dresses, skirts and heels. At first, I felt a little insecure and wanted to give up. People stared at me, but it was something I had to get used to. I had to get comfortable with being seen as my new self.

Wearing makeup became a part of my self-care routine; I was doing it for me. It actually gave me extra confidence. I was showing up to life looking my absolute best. Nothing wrong with that.

As time went on, I became more comfortable taking myself out on dates to nice restaurants (eating at a table for one is no big deal), the cinema and opera. I wanted to treat myself the way I expected a man to treat me. Over time, I became at ease being in my own presence. I was starting to fall in love with myself. I realised I was enough.

That's the magic that happens when you start putting all your time and energy back into yourself. You learn how to refuel yourself with your own cup of love. You learn to speak kind words of encouragement to yourself on a daily basis. You learn that you are the love of your life. I got so carried away with dating myself, I didn't even worry about dating anymore. I was still attracting guys, but I found myself no longer wasting my time on the ones that weren't serious.

Keeping up the momentum

It had been nine months since I had written my manifestation down. I was feeling jet lagged from another solo trip to the USA. It was a nice warm day in Paris, so I decided to get out and go for a walk. I walked around the Opéra Paris, and I remember thinking, "It would be so wonderful to be walking hand-in-hand right now with someone who truly loves me." I was trying to get into that feeling, but I felt a little doubtful and wondered if love would ever happen for me.

That night, I got a message from a friend of mine who had also been travelling. She was back in Paris and invited me to her birthday party the following day. The afternoon before the party, I hung out with some friends until the early evening. I was still feeling the jet lag and wondered if I should just go home to sleep. But a voice inside told me I should go and have a good time.

Less than an hour after being at the party, I went to get drinks at the bar. And that's when my manifestation said hello. We only had three days to get to know each other before he took an eleven-hour flight back home to his island. But during those three days, it was clear we had both connected with each other on a deep level. Our connection is strong, and we can still feel each other's presence even when we're miles apart. It's as if I were taken from his flesh, and he feels like home to me every time he holds me.

Looking back with no regrets

I now write this as a thirty-year-old woman. Looking back over my dating experiences, I forgive myself for not knowing any better. I never really had any good examples of what healthy dating is supposed to be like. Bad experiences made me question my self-worth. I was just trying to figure it all out.

Throughout my twenties, I met other lost women with low self-esteem. They were willing to compromise their time, energy and youth trying to build a man up, when it was never their job in the first place. No man is worth our mental health and wellbeing.

If you find yourself in repeated situation-ships or in unhealthy relationships, the best thing you can do for yourself is decide to achieve your highest potential. Work on your self-esteem, set healthy boundaries, and get to know your higher self. Your higher self will never allow you to stay in situation-ships or unhealthy relationships; it will always want what's best for you. This is what I tell my clients now.

And this is what I would tell my younger self...

Dear Younger Abbey,

The right man will take you out on dates, take his time getting to know you, and will call you back. The right man will never manipulate you or make you question if you're doing something wrong. He will never make you prove that you are worthy of his time and attention. The right man will want to make you happy and give you ALL his love. You are enough, and you deserve love.

Love,
Your older, wiser self

About the Author

Abbey Kelly is an author and life and love strategist.

I help people overcome their limiting beliefs and self-doubts. Through my coaching, we can unblock what's holding you back so that you can at last manifest the life and love you truly want, without any doubts, worry or fear. There is always a strategy for life and love. You've just got to have the right attitude about yourself first.

Visit my website: www.coachabbey.com

Connect with me on Instagram: @abbeyhere

Your Relationship Inventory

Use the worksheets below to examine the impact your most significant relationships have had on you. Use this for your parents individually and other significant caretakers from childhood, your siblings, coaches, first crush, first love, and other intimate relationships that have left an impact on you.

If your discover limiting beliefs or wounds that those relationships left you with, highlight them so you can work on healing them and putting them into a healthy perspective in subsequent exercises.

Name of Person

How I felt around them	
How they treated me	
What I believed about myself due to their treatment	
What attracted me to them	
What I liked about them or how they treated me	
What I disliked about them	
What worked in the relationship	
Why we broke up	
Lessons learned	

Name of Person

How I felt around them	
How they treated me	
What I believed about myself due to their treatment	
What attracted me to them	
What I liked about them or how they treated me	
What I disliked about them	
What worked in the relationship	
Why we broke up	
Lessons learned	

Name of Person

How I felt around them	
How they treated me	
What I believed about myself due to their treatment	
What attracted me to them	
What I liked about them or how they treated me	
What I disliked about them	
What worked in the relationship	
Why we broke up	
Lessons learned	

Chapter 2
Your Attachment Style

Have you ever wondered about what forms the basis for how you show up in the world and how it affects your relationships? Understanding your attachment style can show you why you encountered problems that can be avoided in the future. And most importantly, it may explain a lot about why you may have attracted the wrong people in the past.

The theory of attachment was originally developed by John Bowlby, a British psychoanalyst who wanted to understand the intense distress experienced by infants who had been separated from their parents. Bowlby observed that separated infants would go to extraordinary lengths to prevent separation from their parents or to reestablish proximity to a missing parent. His research, and that of his successors, has given us extraordinary insight into adult attachment styles.

As with so many things about our adult lives, the patterns for how we live were established during our childhood. According to attachment theory, the emotional environment and the kind of care you received as a child influences the psychological connection made between you and your parents or caregivers. The way your primary caregivers attended to your needs as a child created a blueprint for how you experience your needs throughout life, and how you seek to meet them.

Your attachment style involves a pattern of behaviors that appear in relationships in general as well as to your significant other. Understanding why you have the style that you do can provide valuable information about yourself.

As it pertains to romantic relationships, your attachment style dictates whether you feel secure and content, insecure and clingy, or avoidant and dismissive with your partner. In this chapter we will explore how your attachment style impacts your attraction to partners, along with other influences, so that you can be mindful and aware of the conscious choices you make as you embark on your manifesting journey.

This is all about becoming more self-aware in order to consciously manifest the love that you want and deserve. While I know that delving into the past can be uncomfortable, I can tell you for sure that doing this work, reflecting, learning and growing is the key to a brighter future — in your love life and in other areas too.

Also, you will likely find that while your love life improves, so do your other relationships. Friends, family, work; even how lucky you seem to be in everyday life will get a positive boost. Working through your pain will pay off in unexpected ways! You see, when you are more conscious you are more in control of what you manifest for yourself.

The trick of course is to visit your past just long enough to do the work. You don't want to unpack your bags and stay there for too long. So there will be no dwelling and no pity parties. We are going to roll up our sleeves, look at your attachment style, and then move on, armed with the information we need to manifest your next healthy relationship.

Where needs begin

From the moment we are born, we are helpless and dependent. As infants, we seek out our mother (or other primary caregiver) to keep us fed, hydrated, warm, and safe. This is the very beginning of dependence, when we require the presence of another person to make us feel safe — the subconscious lesson here is that being alone is bad, or a threat to our survival. Because human infants, like other mammalian infants, cannot feed or protect ourselves, we are dependent upon the care and protection of "older and wiser" adults.

Infants will display what Bowlby called attachment behaviors when separated by their caregiver. Crying and searching for the caregiver were necessary for survival of the infant. So these behaviors are a part of our nature. And they continue into adulthood.

The way we were treated during the first months of life sets our attachment pattern, which typically remains stable over time, but it can change through different life experiences. While we are in our first few years of life, the neurons in our brain are forming connections at the fastest rate they ever will in our lifetime. The formation of synaptic connections, in simple terms, is the basis of learning. We are forming our blueprint for who we are, what the world is all about, and our place in it. Our attachment pattern created brain pathways and reactive behaviors which impact the development of our self-esteem, our ability to express emotions, our ability to trust others and whether we feel comfortable in establishing intimacy.

We create our sense of self and adopt behaviors to get our needs met early in childhood. Of course, our sense of who we are evolves and finesses over the years into adulthood. But these early years form the building blocks, the foundations if you will. And these building blocks are important parts of us to explore.

The foundation of attachment theory

When attachment theory was first introduced by John Bowlby in 1969, he described attachment as a biological hardwired instinct to seek physical and emotional closeness with caregivers. According to Bowlby, attachment provides a secure base from which the child can explore the environment. The parent or caregiver becomes a haven of safety to which the child can return when he or she is afraid or fearful. Bowlby's colleague Mary Ainsworth recognized that whether a child will have a secure or insecure attachment depends upon the degree of sensitivity shown by their caregiver.

The attachment system internally asks the following fundamental question: Is my attachment figure nearby, accessible, and attentive? If the child perceives the answer to this question to be "yes," he or she feels loved, secure, and confident, and they are likely to explore his or her environment, play with others, and be sociable. If, however, the child perceives the answer to this question to be "no," the child experiences anxiety and is likely to exhibit attachment behaviors, which could be visually searching or actively following and vocally signaling (crying or calling out to the parent/caregiver.) These behaviors continue until either the child is able to reestablish a desired level of physical or psychological closeness to the attachment figure, or until the child "wears down," as may happen in the context of a prolonged separation or loss.

You may not cry like a baby, but even today you may engage in other behaviors to protest the absence of your partner, or to signal that you need affection.

The origins of typing infants' attachment style

In the 1970's developmental psychologist Mary Ainsworth, a colleague of Bowlby, created an experiment known as the Strange Situation Procedure. In the experiment, 12-month old infants were put in an unfamiliar playroom full of toys with their caregiver, most often the mother, for 20 minutes. Researchers observing through a one-way mirror could see how the child reacted to different separation scenarios.

In one scenario, a research assistant that the child had never seen before would enter the room and speak to the parent. The stranger would interact with the child and then the parent would leave the room with the child left with the stranger. The stranger would continue to interact with the infant. The parent would return to the room, comfort the child then leave again.

In a second scenario after parent and infant were in the experiment room, a stranger enters and interacts with parent and child. The stranger leaves, then the parent leaves the child alone. The stranger returns and interacts with the child. The parent enters, greets the infant, and picks up infant and the stranger leaves conspicuously.

There are four aspects of the child's behavior which were observed during the Strange Situation Procedure:

1) The amount of exploration the child engaged in throughout, such as playing with toys.
2) The child's reactions to the departure of its caregiver.
3) The stranger anxiety (when the infant is alone with the stranger).
4) The child's reunion behavior with its caregiver.

On the basis of their behaviors, the children were categorized into three groups, or attachment styles. (A fourth group was added years later.) Each of these groups reflects a different kind of attachment relationship with the caregiver.

The 4 styles of attachment

Secure

In the Strange Situation, roughly 60% of children become upset when the parent leaves the room, but, when he or she returns, they actively seek the parent and are easily comforted by him or her. They are thought to have a secure attachment style, which is developed when a child is regularly attended to, seen, soothed and has consistent warm contact with a sensitive and responsive caregiver. This leads to an adult who has a positive view of themselves, others and relationships.

In the Strange Situation Procedure, the secure child explores and plays freely with the parent present as a secure 'base'. They will engage with the stranger, show signs that they are upset when the parent leaves the room, but they are able to settle themselves down.

The child's assumption is that the caregiver will return and they are happy when the parent returns.

With a secure attachment style one has an underlying belief that "I matter, my needs and feelings matter, my loved ones will keep me safe" because that is what their life has shown them up to that point. They communicate their feelings freely because their caregiver was open to them, and they have learned to regulate their negative emotions in stressful situations.

With secure attachment the brain pathways and structures involved in social and emotional development, communication and relationships grow and develop normally. Because secure partners typically grew up in a family where their needs were met in an appropriate way as often as possible, as adults, these people make well-rounded and supportive partners, who are comfortable with asking for help. They tend to be comfortable with intimacy and make romantic ties easily.

Securely attached adults will make you feel comfortable, they don't divulge too much or too little personal info when they first meet you, and they're not quick to judge you or test you. They are not afraid of being alone for periods of time. And they are not anxious or suspicious about being abandoned.

Insecure

In the Strange Situation, if the attachment figure (parent or primary caregiver) has been inconsistent, insensitive, rejecting or abusive, then the child shows signs of insecurity and will either express anxiety or avoidance behaviors when the parent leaves. If this resonates with you, then think back to your childhood relationship with your caregiver. Were they inconsistent? Did they pull the rug from under you? Did a parent leave, or withhold affection in some way?

There are three subtypes of insecure attachment styles described in the research.

Anxious-avoidant

In the Strange Situation Procedure, the anxious-avoidant infant ignores or avoids the caregiver, does not explore and play with toys, does not show signs of distress when the caregiver leaves, and ignores the caregiver when they return. They may have approached the caregiver when they reentered the room, only to turn away from them.

Researchers found that the anxious-avoidant type experienced frequent rejection as children. Either their needs were met inconsistently, or their cries were responded to infrequently. Their requests for attention may have been met with refusal, annoyance, or even anger. They may have been shamed for wanting attention.

It was theorized that the child came to believe that communicating their needs had no influence on the caregiver. Sometimes referred to as 'dismissive' the child would try to keep a close enough distance for safety, but far away enough to avoid rebuff. This typically results in the child learning to pull back and emotionally shut themselves off — mainly to avoid further hurt.

As adults, those with the avoidant attachment style avoid getting too close, they often refuse to rely much on their romantic partners and often see those partners as "needy" if they require too much intimacy. Avoidant people tend to equate intimacy with a loss of independence and constantly try to minimize closeness. As an adult, being an avoidant type can mean that you expect nothing to be guaranteed and that things could be taken away from you at a moment's notice. Maybe you are always on guard, wondering when the next disappointment would come.

Can you see this pattern in yourself or in previous partners? People with the anxious-avoidant style often find it hard to say the words, "I love you", although they may show love in other ways. Other signs include shutting down emotionally, or mentally checking out when things get tough. They many not want to get too close in the first place, having little trust for other people.

Anxious-preoccupied

This style basically boils down to being clingy, needy, or highly anxious. With this attachment pattern one is often preoccupied with their relationships and tend to worry about their partner's ability to love them back. The root cause is typically inconsistent parenting. A sense that the love or attention received in childhood was conditional or based on their caregivers' mood.

In the Strange Situation Procedure the infant showed distress even **before** the caregiver left the room. They were wary of strangers, even with the parent present. They were clingy and difficult to comfort. When the parent was out of the room they either showed signs of resentment or became passive and helpless. The behavior strategy adopted is a response to unpredictable caregiving. The displays of anger or helplessness towards the caregiver when they reentered the room were seen as a conditional strategy for maintaining the availability of the caregiver by preemptively taking control of the interaction.

The trouble with the inconsistent care is that you never know what to expect — hence the anxiety. This typically manifests as a need to keep your parents, and later in life your partner, close to you. Very, very close to you.

Have you ever been told you are clingy, or 'too much'?

Other signs to look out for are things like being hypersensitive to tiny changes in your partner's mood. For example, maybe driving in heavy traffic has stressed your partner out, but you tend to interpret that as them being mad at you. And, if you find that you live for validation from others, then this may be a sign of your anxious attachment style at work.

Disorganized or fearful-avoidant attachment style

In the Strange Situation, a child with a disorganized attachment expresses odd or ambivalent behavior toward the parent, such as initially running up to them, then immediately pulling away, perhaps even running away from the parent, curling up in a ball or hitting the parent. The child's first impulse may be to seek comfort from the parent, but as they get near the parent, they feel fear to be close to them.

This is the most common attachment style for children of abuse or those whose parents suffered some sort of loss or trauma. Having experiences of abuse, neglect or unresolved trauma in one's early life can have lasting residue that leaves a parent prone to being flooded by emotions in times of stress between them and their child.

If you grew up in a highly stressful, traumatizing environment, then consider this…

Was your primary caregiver also somebody you feared? Did you come to realize that there was no consistent way to get your needs met?

When your parent of guardian is also your abuser or negligent, you don't know where to turn to get your needs met. Your source of safety is also your source of pain.

As adults, if they suffered abuse, researchers find that they may offer unusual explanations for their abuser's behavior. When they're asked to share details of their relationship with their parents, their stories are fragmented, and they have difficulty expressing themselves clearly.

A person who grew up with a disorganized attachment often won't learn healthy ways to soothe themselves when stressed. They may struggle in social situations or find it difficult in co-regulating their emotions with others. Some may find it difficult to open up to others or to seek out help. They often have difficulty trusting people, as they were unable to trust those they relied on for safety growing up. They often struggle in their relationships or friendships or when parenting their own children.

This is you if you crave closeness but also fear or reject it at the same time. In your rational mind, you know that love exists in this world for you. But trusting somebody enough to experience that love feels too risky, so you stay closed off or emotionally unavailable.

Further exploration

The tricky thing about all of these attachment styles is that while we are unconscious to them, we can absolutely kid ourselves that what we are doing is completely functional. If we have never explored this topic, then we don't know any better.

So when we are avoidant and our partner says we are cold, we tell ourselves it's our partner who is wrong. "*They* must be too needy – I'm doing my best, what more do they want?"

But when we can see the pattern with perspective, and own our part in the whole dance of our attachment style interacting with our partner's style, then we can make conscious choices about staying and working together, or moving on to new pastures. As to which is more appropriate for you, well, that's for you to decide. But what I wish for you to get from this book is the belief that your dreams of a conscious, loving relationship are within reach, because I truly believe that they are.

By becoming conscious of our patterns and making better decisions, we are vibrating higher and actively telling the Universe what we desire — instead of anxiously telling it what we fear! We are now in a much better position to manifest our hearts' desire.

If you have found this very short summary of attachment styles thought provoking and you can tell you have some unresolved issues that have triggered uncontrollable behaviors in times past, I highly recommend you read *Attached* by Amir Levine, MD and Rachel Heller. It provides a thorough explanation of the how our attachment styles appear in adult relationships with a comprehensive roadmap for managing different combinations of attachment styles.

Chapter 3
Uncover The Blocks to Giving and Receiving Love

Unhealed Wounds

The painful experiences of our past can linger in our brains and bodies for years, and even entire lifetimes. The unhealed wounds of the past, whether conscious or unconscious, can create immense barriers to intimacy, connection and lasting relationship harmony. And we can easily delude ourselves about their significance.

Recently, I was hit hard with the realization that the disappointments from my recent relationships weren't healed completely. Sitting on the edge of my bed one morning, I burst into tears, full of fear and despair. The thought in my mind rang out with pitiful weariness, "What if I never get it right?!"

I had just started communicating with a man I met through a dating app. He was handsome, well spoken, charming and seemingly genuine in his interest in me. There were no obvious red flags that he was only looking for casual conversation. And I doubted he was looking for quick intimacy as we were 1000 kilometers apart.

We had talked, texted, or sent voice messages every day since our first connection 3 weeks ago. He even admitted that he had paused his account n the appo so as to avoid being distracted. Apparently he wanted to focus on getting to know me.

So why the tears?

A faint, tentative voice asked "What if I never get it right?" I knew the voice of my inner child. But never had I ever heard this question from her. It soon made sense as images flowed through my mind of the last guy I opened my heart to. With him I felt that I was my 'best self', and despite open vulnerability and honest dialogue, we ended our brief courtship because the intensity of love and fear of being hurt triggered us both with uncomfortable force.

Then the memories of the man I deeply connected with last year came to mind. With him I shared myself openly, I was generously loving and hopeful for a future with him. But it to came to an abrupt end when he admitted that he didn't know what he was doing with his life. Though he had been divorced for over 5 years, he had been with his wife since his early twenties and he said he had no clue how to be in a relationship.

Looking back on that brief encounter, I realized that he had shown multiple signs that he really wasn't in a position to be in the kind of co-committed partnership that I want. Why did I ignore those signs? Why didn't I step back or get out? I couldn't even blame him. I can clearly see his messy midlife awakening for what it was. His inability to show up for me wasn't a reflection on how worthless I thought myself to be, it was his state of being at the time.

But on the day the unprovoked tears dripped from my eyes I could feel the self-blame and shame overpower me. I sobbed as I realized why it made sense to be struck with such fear. Having a bit of time behind me after those past 2 breakups I felt ready to try again. So, with this new potential partner I allowed myself to hope again. The wounded me was feeling shaky and worried that the disappointment and pain might knock me down again.

As I wept into my pillow I reminded my inner child that she is lovable. I whispered over and over, "I love you. I love you. I love you. And no matter what happens, there is a man who will love and accept you as your are."

My self-comforting continued, " You don't have to be anything other than what you are today." I could hear the protest rise in my ears, "But who would want to be with someone who feels so scared of being hurt that she cries for no reason? No man is gonna want an insecure woman!"

Before those thoughts solidified I immediately said, "You are lovable and the *right* partner will be perfectly matched to you. He will recognize, accept and love you in your humanness. And he will be so happy to have you as his queen that he won't see any of your fears or doubts as burdens or imperfections."

My inner monologue continued to comfort me. "You've had some experiences that have been painful and they've caused you to be fearful and suspicious. That's understandable. They've made you think that you're bad, deserving of blame, or that somehow you've brought the pain on yourself. But it isn't true. Yes, you've played a part in the experiences, but you are not to blame. You have always done your best. You deserve compassion and forgiveness."

And with those sentiments floating through my mind, I felt my heart begin to lift from the dark cloud of sadness. I held myself tight and said, "You are human. You've been hurt, and you've also hurt others. But you do not need to keep suffering. Forgive yourself. Forgive those who have hurt and disappointed you. You're ready to move forward without fear."

Being conscious of the heartbreak and disappointments of our past doesn't mean we have to be suspicious, fearful or protective forever. In fact, being aware of the wounds can help us shine light on our hearts, engage in the healing work of self-compassion, and when needed, look for clues as to why the heartbreak happened in the first place.

Be sure to download the guided meditation audios at ManifestingLoveBook.com to bring healing attention to those old wounds.

Unspoken Expectations

Do you have ideals about how men and women should behave in relationships? For example, is a man supposed to be the financial supporter, the home repair man and car maintainer while the woman is a homemaker, meal preparer, and supportive caretaker? Do you feel that the man is meant to be the pursuer and the woman the pursued? Believing in outdated gender roles may set you up for relationship strife if your partner has other beliefs.

Just as important as roles and responsibilities is the way that you show love. According to Gary Chapman, author of *The Five Love Languages: How to Express Heartfelt Commitment to Your Mate*, we each give and receive love in our own language. In other words, we have preferred ways of being shown that we are loved and sometimes they differ from the ways our partners typically show love. When we learn to speak our partner's love language, there is the possibility for deeper connection, true harmony and lasting intimacy.

The five ways of expressing love include: words of affirmation, physical touch, gifts, acts of service and quality time. You can take a short quiz to determine your love language by visiting www.5lovelanguages.com

Many divorced people have told me that in the beginning of their marriages there was a lot of affection and they felt loved. But over time the little moments of disconnection, busyness with kids or work led to dissatisfaction with the relationship. Many times that they discovered that they simply didn't have the same love language. One woman really felt that her partner taking out the trash without being asked made her feel supported and loved. (That's an act of service.) While he says that the gentle back rubs she used to give him when the first got together made him feel loved. (Physical touch). Over time those little displays were fewer and farther between, leading each of them to feeling less loved.

Looking over your past relationships, what sorts of things made you feel loved, secure and cared for? What was missing? If you take the quiz and discover your primary love language, and learn about the language of your past partners (and even your parents or caretakers), you may find that you can consciously ask for what you want and be more open to giving your future partner what they want in the way they want it.

Mismatched Attachment Styles

As explained in the previous chapter, your attachment style impacts the way you show up in relationship and can create challenges between you and your partner.

If you have an anxious attachment style you may tend to overanalyze your partner's behavior, second-guess their feelings toward you, and worry that they may abruptly lose interest and end the relationship. As you find yourself frequently preoccupied with your relationships or uncertain of whether your partner *really* loves you, or you worry that they will leave you, you may act out in ways that conflict with your partner. Remember that infants with anxious attachment styles display protest behaviors when their attachment figure leaves, including crying, clinging, and frantically searching for them. As an adult you may exhibit nervous tendencies to keep close tabs on your partner with frequent calling, asking for more time together or on the severe side, sneaking into their phones or emails to check if they've been unfaithful. You may find greatest harmony with someone who has a secure attachment style. Getting into relationship with someone who can respond to your needs without getting defensive will be ideal.

Of course, not all adults with the anxious attachment style will resort to behaviors that border on the stalker or detective, but those who do these things will find that their partners may not be able to tolerate much of it. Someone with a secure attachment style, who is open, empathetic and interested in maintaining a relationship may understand your behaviors and see them for what they are. Particularly if you had early childhood experiences that led to a clingy or anxious style.

Alternatively, a person who also has an anxious attachment style may be overly sensitive, seeing your behavior as a sign that they cannot trust you to be the secure base they desire in relationship. You may find that the one of you is always working to reassure the other or you're in endless rupture-repair cycles.

Someone with an avoidant or dismissive attachment style could present quite a challenge to an anxiously attached person. While the avoidant needs space, especially after periods of intimacy or closeness, the anxious person may prefer even more closeness and connection than is tolerable for the avoidant.

With enough emotional intelligence any combination of the 4 styles of attachment could mix, mingle and have lasting love relationships. It may require a great deal of patience, tolerance, compassion and honest communication. The secure attachment types are really adaptable which means that can provide the intimacy and reassurance that anxious and fearful partners require without getting unnerved; they can also provide those with an avoidant style with the space they need, so romantic relationships don't overwhelm them.

So it is wise to be aware of these tendencies so that as you imagine your ideal future with your beloved, you see yourself behaving and being treated in the ways that will bring you security, harmony and happiness. Amir Levine, co-author of *Attached* developed a quick way to evaluate your potential partner. He suggest you look for "CARRP," which means a person who is consistent, available, reliable, responsive and predictable. Do they make time to go on dates? Do they answer the phone when you call? Do they respond to your texts in a timely manner? And when you express needs in the relationship needs, are they met with compassion?

Chapter 4
Essential Elements for Manifesting

There are some essential ingredients that are included in many successful manifesting rituals and ceremonies which the stories in this section highlight. But even the accidental or coincidental connections leave clues for you to follow. We begin with setting your intention and envisioning what you most desire to experience and feel in your relationship. Of course to call forth a partner you want to show the universe (and your potential partner) that you have the time and space for them in your life or home.

Even when you have addressed past hurts and disappointments there may still be some resistance or fear to clear before opening your heart, mind and home to sharing your life with someone. How can you be sure that the one who steps forth is really the best match for you? Can you trust? Are you ready? You really need to explore these questions.

Even with all the preparation in the world, there still comes a moment when you must surrender with faith that the force of love and the Universe itself will guide you to the best match for your soul's growth. Finally, when you want to make a clear declaration to the Universe, the soul of your beloved and your higher self, engaging in a formal ritual or personal ceremony to manifest your relationship may give you the confidence you need to let go of trying to control the process.

In this chapter you will read stories of 7 more authors who have used these essential manifesting elements to attract their soul mate.

Vision & Intention

Creating a relationship vision is a beautiful starting point in your manifesting process. Consider the answers to these questions. How do you want to be treated in relationship? How much closeness are you comfortable with? How will you treat your partner? How will you pass the years together?

Imagine, in full sensory delight, how it will look and feel to be in relationship with your beloved. What will you do together? What does time alone look like? How much will you go out and socialize alone or together? How often do you see yourselves traveling and to which destinations?

What does the intimate aspect of your relationship look like in your ideal vision? What about family? And have you considered where you want to live and whether you are open to relocating?

And, being realistic, we know there will be conflicts in our relationships. Can you imagine how the two of you will resolve them? Given your attachment style, how will you relate to your partner's need for intimacy, closeness or distance and alone time?

If you could describe the day in the life of you and your beloved, how would it start and end? In the ideal week, month or year, how does the dynamic unfold? Having a clear vision of the things you most desire will get you in the right headspace and set the tone for the vibration you emit to the Universe.

As Abbey's story from Chapter 1 detailed, being clear about the things that are **not** included in your vision is equally important. We attract what we focus on. So when we complain about things or focus on negative traits we will often see even more of them around us! Therefore we need to send a clear signal about the positive aspects we wish to attract. So rather than saying what you don't want, such as I don't want a smoker, I don't want someone who is late, avoidant, dismissive, or only out for superficial relating, you should imagine and describe the opposite, in positive language.

For example, at one of our self-love retreats one beautiful soul shared her relationship vision with our group, and she agreed to have it shared here.

She wrote:

My beloved and I wake up and have time for snuggles and intimacy before the day fully begins. Sometimes I wake for early morning yoga and come back to bed as he is waking up. Either way, we always make time to connect physically, whether making love or not, before leaving the bed to start our day.

After meditating or breathing together, we set our intentions for the day. Then we enjoy a light breakfast together, sometimes the kids are with us — being busy teenagers it's not always possible! We shower and head out to our respective work places.

He sends me sweet voice messages and photos during the day to stay connected. And I share what I'm up to as well via text or video message. We speak on the phone for lunch if it's a day we don't eat together.

We meet at home in the evening and prepare a meal together, which our kids join. There is a loving, open and happy vibe at the dinner table as we catch up on the day's activities. We enjoy a relaxed evening at home most of the time, but occasionally we go out dancing or meet friends in town. He is always sending little glances or seductive winks my way, and I love it!

We maintain our connection with regular date nights without the kids. We travel abroad together each year with our children and alone. We visit our aging parents often and we stay healthy, fit and active.

He is affectionate, shares his innermost feelings, dreams and ambitions with me, and I with him. He is my best friend and often says that I am his best friend. He surprises me with handwritten cards, gifts and trips to keep me guessing what he'll do next!

We have plans to work on projects together, investing our time and energy into mutually stimulating causes. We continuously work on our individual growth as well as our development as a couple and family.

Reading this vision helped her imagine how she will behave with her beloved. I could totally see them taking trips and enjoying their blended family. It was also inspiring to see how reading the vision lit her eyes up!

Take some time to write your own relationship vision. Be as detailed and specific as you want, and don't be afraid to dream big. You are actively setting an intention for the type of relationship you will manifest, which also serves as a standard-setting document against which you can evaluate a new partner's compatibility.

While it's not a 100% foolproof method, the Universe often knows what's best for us, it can be a useful starting point. As you'll read in the next story, Karan and Eric set their intentions and had visions in mind that didn't totally match the reality they live today. But it at least put them into the mindset to manifest their soulmate relationship.

Accidentally on Purpose

By Karan Joy Almond & Eric Gerson

The Universe plays cupid

After his marriage of 24 years came to an end, he sat at his desk and with abundant skepticism, scrolled through the dating site. Sixteen pages later, having found only one remote possibility, he logged off the site. He was immediately presented with pop-up ads and a site for spiritual singles caught his attention. Half blind and exhausted from a full day of online work, he created a profile, attaching the one and only digital picture of himself he was comfortable sharing. To this day, he still cannot recall what he wrote. He pressed submit and headed to bed with three hundred collective pounds of dog, content that they may be his ideal companions.

While he was sleeping, she was wide awake and feeling the loneliness of losing her beloved dogs to her ex-husband. To pass the hours, she opened her laptop to finish up some emails but was distracted by an ad for a dating website that invited her to check out the spiritual singles in her area. Feeling pessimistic, she reluctantly opened the email to see if anyone out there might meet her need for companionship. Something happened that she did not expect. The man in the very first profile she saw had eyes that she felt she recognized, but she closed the laptop and took it upstairs. Once in bed, the absence of her four-legged companions prompted her to reopen her laptop and read his profile. He had her at "must love dogs." For the small fee of $39.99, she sent a quick message acknowledging she was out of his stated age range, closed her laptop, and went to bed thinking how silly she was acting for a woman her age.

After spending the month of August walking circles around his fire pit, with the deliberate intention of manifesting the woman of his dreams, he opened his email to find a message from the dating site he hardly recalled signing up for the previous evening. Multiple times, over the course of his manifesting ritual, Spirit had presented a clear vision of her appearance, so he instantly recognized her face upon seeing the picture attached to her message. He laughed at her email in which she used a predetermined disqualifier based on their age difference, and immediately decided to challenge her assumption.

Little did he know that she had spent the month of August manifesting as well, just in an entirely different manner. Her approach to manifesting the man of her dreams was not as intentional as it was accidental, since she had been steadfast in her decision that she would never "settle" again. But she would soon realize that she was ready to open her heart to the right partner. Even though she felt curious excitement upon awakening to his response the following morning, she would have thought she was delusional had she known then that a man 10 years her junior, whose picture picked at the edges of hormones she had long since forgotten, would be clamoring to crawl into her backseat on the first date (teaser for our upcoming book?, lol.) Still, she made a conscious choice to respond to his challenge, pressed send, and the story of Eric and Karan began.

Magic is possible without a magic formula

Our story is a prime example of how two people can manifest the same outcome in very different ways. The point is, there is no magic formula. For example, Eric lives on three beautiful acres surrounded by nature. The fenced portion of his property was where he spent many hours in silent meditative peace with his three dogs. His daily practice began with a glass vessel of water that he would lift to the sun, while asking for his desire. Once the sun filled the water with the energy of that request, the water would be consumed, and he would begin his process, which also had no magic formula.

Yes, it may have seemed random, but Eric would listen for Spirit to guide the actions of his physical body. There were times he would practice his trademark "sun squinting" in which he would begin to see small streaks of colored light. It was at this point that the visions would appear. There were other times when Eric would walk deliberate small clockwise circles around his fire pit and times he would walk larger circles around the trees on his property, always attempting to keep the dogs inside the circle so they would be included in the manifestation of the woman he knew would come.

At the same time, Karan had pondered whether she was the common denominator in her three failed marriages. Still, her desire for a specific type of partner was palpable, as evidenced by her journal writings over the previous decade. For as many years, she had attended workshops, retreats, and spiritual events alone, attempting to transform her relationships to meet her strong desire to feel connected. The trouble was, she had attempted to change the partners she had settled for. By the time she had successfully rebuilt her health and career, the last thread of her marriage had unraveled, concurrent with acknowledging and giving voice to her desire for an authentic life and soul connection with a partner.

During the same month that Eric had begun manifesting the woman of his dreams, Karan realized that the only thing left to do was to sit still, envision what it would feel like if she got what she wanted, and wait for the timing of the universe to present it. So, she engaged in guided meditations for two hours each day during the month of August. The chakra alignment meditations put her in a place of such peace that she began to have out-of-body experiences where she came to the realization that she had been blocking her entire life by taking action before the universe could!

Resistance is futile

Spontaneous and hilarious text communications between Eric and Karan were exchanged, but it soon became abundantly clear that getting to know each other would require an actual "hands-on" experience. While Karan spent the weeks leading up to their first date giving Eric every reason why he would not want a long-term committed relationship with her, Eric spent his time responding with, "Is that all you got?" He began setting the boundaries he knew would be necessary for any woman to consider in moving forward in a committed relationship with him.

One would think that after what Eric described as the "best last first date ever," they would both find comfort in dropping their guard. However, they both intensified their attempt to sabotage their relationship due to Eric's fear that no woman would be willing or able to tolerate the life that would inevitably come as a package deal, and Karan's fear that her one, slash two, slash three, slash four, slash FIVE previous relationships were evidence that she was not long-term relationship material. This did not inhibit the strong connection they felt, but it became obvious that a long-distance text relationship would be doomed to the hell fires of failure. Even though they lived in the same state and only 90 minutes apart, they were separated by Maryland's Bay Bridge which posed a block to the normal dating process. This was due to Eric's demands at home and his extreme vertigo, which made bridge travel dangerous for him and others, not to mention seasonal weekend traffic that could stretch a ninety-minute trip into two hours!

This is where they began to understand that manifesting a desire does not mean there is not more work to do. Relationships are where we learn the most about ourselves and theirs was no different, except they were clearly being shown that this would be about Spirit's timing rather than theirs. Karan wanted Spirit's assurance that a move to the other side of the bridge would not recreate her pattern of previous relationship dynamics, but Eric stood with his feet planted, acknowledging what he wanted and waiting for Karan to accept what she already knew.

Even though Eric knew he had manifested Karan, the reality of his day-to-day life presented challenges to Karan's ability to make the choice to move — the least of which was Eric's love of hockey and his commitment to hockey video recaps until his team made the playoffs. Karan's profile had clearly drawn some red lines in the sand with "no sports" at the top of that list. Turned out, red lines in the sand were the least of our challenges, as events would rapidly repeat themselves until we made a choice to turn around and walk away from them, together.

Love is a choice: Triggers, communication, and healing

Over a short period of time, we noticed a pattern in our communication when an unexpected external event would present. The cycle played out something like this. First, one of us would find ourselves triggered by an external source. For example, communicating with an ex or unwittingly uttering a phrase the other had heard one too many times before. Subconsciously, the energy of that person would shift, leading them to become resistant or defensive while the other was spinning in confusion and doing whatever it took to gain clarity. Since we had so many similar past experiences, we both had the patience to just stand still, even though we were spinning in place, and allow the other to work through whatever it was they were feeling. What developed was a level of trust that allowed the triggered person to feel comfortable enough to begin the process of deep emotional excavation.

Simultaneously, the other person would be forced to dig deep into their own perceptions and responses so that by the end, both of us had experienced deep internal shifts. The gift in that level of self-analysis was the deep intimate conversations that followed, in which we revealed our deepest thoughts, fears, anxieties, and weird idiosyncratic selves at a pace not deemed "normal" in new relationships. Some of these confessions had never been exposed at all over the course of our marriages. Each time this occurred, the process was expedited and deepened to the point that the next cycle would become so intense that there were more than a few moments of asking, "How bad do I really want this?" Each time, the end result had us reconfirming the choice we had made to manifest each other.

This would be followed by another pattern, in which the closeness, trust, and security we felt far surpassed the depth of any past relationship. We were even astonished at how rapidly we were working through and letting go of our pasts. Within just a few months, we had worked through several complex relationship dynamics that we had been unable to work through in our combined 44 years of marriage. This is where it becomes apparent that the level of relationship most people only dream about requires partners to practice what Eric calls, "reverse engineering," where each person goes back in time and recalls the original inciting event from the past to understand what is currently happening in the relationship. It requires a change in what Karan calls the "narrative," in which we make a choice to stop protecting ourselves and become vulnerable enough to change the story. We also make a choice to love our "person" daily. Passion just happens, but love is a choice. That takes work but the pay off can be pretty sweet!

As we are writing this and attempting to find a detailed example of those intense emotional conversations, we are reminded of the stellar job we must have done at clearing out the baggage and putting it behind us. So, we will just share what we believe was the key to letting Spirit know we were doing the work and were ready to move forward to the next level of what would come. Without fail, we would go through our "process" and within hours to a few days, would ask, "So what now?" or "What were we fighting about?"

Perhaps, this was because we were not really fighting with each other, as much as we took turns fighting to prevent the recurrence of past episodes the other person was unaware even existed. Although this did not always precipitate a fight, a simple example is that Eric would often randomly and abruptly respond or end a text with "Bye." Karan was unaware that he was just being his normal sarcastic self, and Eric was unaware of her experience with people in her past abruptly walking away in the middle of a conversation, so she questioned if that was his way of shutting her down. Eric would be completely perplexed at how she arrived at that conclusion.

What we soon realized was that tone and inflection, being absent in text communication, must be taken into consideration. We may be less challenged by that dynamic now, but we have realized that text communication, beyond banter, is not our forte when we are apart. In hindsight, perhaps, Spirit's plan was to force us to realize that a long-term long-distance relationship would not be sustainable if we were to come together to do the work we believe we have been given to do.

Accepting Spirit's timeline

As our connection grew, it became obvious that spiritual work would be a huge part of what we would do together, so much so that at times Karan questioned if the journey would be more about lightwork than a romantic relationship. Eric had been unable to focus his energies due to his familial obligations, but he was a gifted intuitive channeler and distance healer who Karan believed needed a little push to further develop and use those gifts. She once said, "Ya know, it's kinda rude to reject a gift when it is given." He definitely showed Karan this gift in tangible ways, some showing Eric's rascally side, but Karan could write an entire chapter based on that alone! As the relationship grew, Eric's gifts began to multiply exponentially, providing further proof of the invitation to consider melding our abilities in regard to lightwork.

As we stated, despite our antics, our story developed on Spirit's timeline rather than ours. We met and had our last first best date ever in September 2018. A timeline decision was made for Karan's move by the end of January. By March, we were living in the same home due to circumstances we did not predict, and by June, we had begun working on our first book, *How to Survive the 2020 Election by Living a Law of Attraction Life*, published in November 2019. Our plan is to write a book about our relationship with all the juicy details, but the point of this chapter is about knowing what you want and not being afraid to allow it to happen when it arrives. Manifestations rarely happen the way we think they will, but it's important to allow the process to play out, regardless of how uncomfortable it may feel.

While Eric knew he wanted to manifest his dream woman and Karan knew she would never settle for a man she did not have a strong emotional connection with, we both knew that we wanted to be aligned spiritually. We could not have imagined how our new life would come together as the old one dropped away to make room for so much more than we actually asked for.

About the Authors

Eric and Karan offer remote Spirit-driven sessions for Lightworkers and those who are waking up to their own gifts. Together we are a playful energetically in tune couple empowered to guide you to the core of your personal truth with compassion. Eric is an instrument of truth while Karan is an instrument of compassion making us a powerhouse of authenticity!

As Lightworkers, we are intimately familiar with the way Spirit works. The more we open up to offering our gifts to others, the deeper we are required to look within ourselves. We recognize a need for Lightworkers to have a safe place to continue their own growth and development of their gifts. Using a combination of channeled messages, intuition, and elements of Human Design, we act as conduits to help you continue the journey of discovering compassion for yourself while uncovering your authentic truths.

Get in touch with Karan and Eric:
Email: lionsandgoats@lightworkforlightworkers.com

Facebook Group Lightwork for Lightworkers
https://www.facebook.com/groups/937306003443582/

Our YouTube channel can be found by searching "Lightwork for Lightworkers" or at:
https://www.youtube.com/channel/UCUSriMUarxHcqqYBDdNscIg

Space

It may seem obvious, but you need to have ample space in your life, schedule, and heart for a partner before you can effectively attract them. For those who've spent years alone, whether by choice or by circumstance, there's a big chance that you've expanded your activities or work to occupy all of the space in your life, home or mind. A busy schedule, a cluttered bedroom, full closets…all of these put you at risk of not having adequate, welcoming space for your new relationship. This also goes for the superficial relationships that you hang onto as space holders. If you've been maintaining a 'friends with benefits' type of relationship, you won't have the space to welcome a loving, healthy partnership.

Are you pining away for a past relationship? If your heart is partially occupied by a previous lover, you need to energetically release them so you have room in your heart for your beloved. If someone left you, abused you or rejected you, then you need to accept their choice and move on. Holding space for them will be counterproductive. And would you really want them back anyway?

This doesn't mean you have to cut all memories of passed loves out, unless they are holding your back from welcoming new love. For example if your husband or wife passed away and you have no reason to eliminate them from your heart or mind, you can simply move the place you hold to what Gabriel Gonsalves calls a 'special chamber' in your mind, but open up space in your heart for your new partner.

Finally, if you've felt isolated and lonely for a long time, you may have plenty of space for a new partner in your life, but I invite you to explore whether that space is tidy and inviting. Is your living space open to share with your beloved?

In addition to changing furniture and adding personal touches of your own, many people find that burning white sage in their living space can clear out old energies from previous inhabitants and past relationships. Add to your manifestation process envisioning how you and your beloved will be in the space together.

As you'll read in the next story, Lene found that the home she once shared with her ex-husband didn't have a very welcoming vibe for a new partner. Her use of Feng Shui, the ancient art of placement, helped her to establish a new personal energy in her home. This was significant in her preparations for entering into a new life partnership.

Essential Elements for Manifesting

Making Room for Love Again

By Lene Nielsen

How I learned that my son had lost both parents due to the divorce, even though only one had moved to the other side of the world.

I always knew that the 1st of January 2013 would be a very special day. I had imagined a day filled with confetti, balloons, and flags. Plates all over the place, favourite music playing, all the clear signs of a party, and the start of a brand new year.

And it was a day full of confetti and balloons, dirty plates and empty glasses on the kitchen counter, and the day after the New Year's Eve. Yet it was nothing like I had imagined...

I was up way too early for the morning after a celebration. No music played, the Scandinavian winter morning darkness and a thick fog surrounded the house.

It was the exact opposite of the celebration I had dreamed of. It could have been the 'copper' wedding anniversary, celebrating 12½ years of marriage with my son's dad. Instead it was the day where my ex-husband arrived on the other side of the world to start a new life with his new wife.

I felt the grief and loss in the stark contrasts that only that particular day could really show so painfully clear. In the darkness of the early morning, I realized that my son had not only lost the privilege of having his dad in his life on a daily basis – he had also lost me.

I had given too much away. I felt empty inside and wasn't able to be present for anyone, not for me, not for my son. I was the one left to take care of him, hold a job to be able to put a roof over our heads and make things work. And on that day, for the first time, I allowed myself to feel totally depleted and unable to do anything.

My self love journey

By now I had been alone with my son for one year. Deep down I knew that getting divorced was the opportunity for me to truly find myself and live the life that I longed for. Being alone with a 5-year-old and all the turmoil of the divorce, standing on my own two shaky feet didn't feel at all like self love at the time. In fact it left me thinking "what have we done" more often than thinking "I know this is my path".

With me being in charge of doing everything around the house I was exhausted and sometimes also felt annoyed. There were some tasks I just did not want to do. Like cleaning. I have to admit that I never liked cleaning in the first place. My ex-husband and I would often clean together. So I really felt alone during those times. Now I had to both initiate the tidying up and then clean, alone. Double trouble and a cocktail consisting of both the practical and the emotional pain.

After a while I started treating myself to do the least annoying housework first, that way I would not be totally fed up before I got half-way through the list of chores. I extended this principle to the list of least favorite things, too. That helped a great deal. But it was not until I found out that I could regain that energy around the cleaning if I hired someone in to clean. Not to clean while I was at work. Instead I arranged for us to clean the house together to reinstate the energy and the feeling of not having to do everything on my own! What a bliss and a beautiful friendship that turned out to be. It was also a celebration of the tiny wins finding their way to me within the four walls of the home.

I am so grateful that I dared to admit to myself that the cleaning work wasn't working out for me. I was able to use my creativity to find a new way forward, my way forward. Actually this also led to my own realization that I was super creative. Wow. Me? Creative? I had never seen myself as creative but the situation was calling for solutions that I had not yet needed or tried. The creativity was a very welcome guest and one that has become a treasured and lifelong friend which continues to take the depth of my self love to new dimensions. Every small step counts. Here's to what I did not want in my life – but what about what I did want in my life?

A friend invited me to a one-day Neo Feng Shui course, and even though I did not feel I had the energy, I really needed to have a day out in great company. I was also curious to learn more about the way we can work intentionally to make our physical surroundings support us. During the course I realized that I didn't even know what I wanted to achieve in the different areas of my life.

Ouch. Can you imagine the fright, the moment you realize that the journey ahead is soo much longer than you ever imagined, and soo much longer than you think you can ever manage?

On that one-day course, luckily a year-long personal development programme was also offered. In this course I was given the chance to explore each of the 9 areas that Feng Shui builds upon and what they represent in my life. Big sigh of relief. So even though I had to wait a year for the course to start – I made the decision to join.

That I dared to own my realization from the first of January that I was not able to be present for myself and my son was significant. Combining that heart-felt realization with the commitment to myself to join the personal development course changed my energy: from not knowing what I desired in my life – to having prioritized the space for me to explore what I really longed for.

I will be forever grateful for giving myself – my inner child, inner man and inner woman – the space and love to grow and develop without working towards a traditional exam. In the beginning, I was challenged enough by loving me and being present with my son.

The learning experience with the group of participants was amazing and I completed year 1, 2 and 3 of the programme. After the three years

I even became a mentor in the 9-step process. The training was based on the constant alternation between helping others and allowing others to hold space for my journey. I gained valuable insights, skills, and most importantly self love. As well as more clarity about what was making me happy and how I could also be more present with myself and with others.

You cannot expect that someone will want to live with you where you have lived with your ex

After a few years I felt I was ready to share my life and love with someone again.

My son and I lived in a big house in the countryside. I dreamed of sharing my life and the house with a man, maybe even with a new family. In that way the house became a symbol of an unrealized dream. The house was where I had also lived with my ex-husband. I had worked on making the house mine over several years – tidying up and decorating it my way. I could feel the shift in my energy when I worked on the house.

Even with the great and helpful personal development journey, life was not smooth sailing at all. Living with a son who missed his dad like crazy is probably one of the most difficult challenges I have ever faced. If you have children or love someone who is dealing with heart-break you know the feeling of devastating powerlessness. I wished that I could just relieve him of his pain. You can help and support someone in pain but you cannot take it away. I knew that it was up to him to find his peace and his way forward.

I decided to give myself a Feng Shui consultation to lift the energies in the house to benefit both my son and myself. I knew the consultant, Lone, and I was ready to work with the things that really, really matter (not just on the surface of things). And because we went through all areas of the house we also touched upon the love in my life – or lack of it.

One of the crystal clear messages I received during the consultation – and one that I will never forget – was that Lone said "You cannot expect that a man would want to live in this house, where you have lived with your ex-husband. You have to work on making this a home for you and your son." Wow... That initially struck me as a big punch to my dream of sharing my life and the house with a man. I soon realized that she was absolutely right and I would also like to choose for myself if I were to live in a house where my new love had lived with his ex.

Focusing on self love and acceptance of the present and having compassion for myself were the key elements in the consultation and the adjustments made afterwards. I say adjustments because with very, very few changes like a new color on one wall in the living room, and re-established balance of the elements in all rooms, especially in my bedroom, the area of Love in the Feng Shui Bagua, the new self love intentions and support for us were manifested.

Meeting someone – a married man

Accepting the appreciation of the now and the manifestations of self love and compassion gave a magnificent sense of freedom and zest for life. I started thinking that someone I had met one year earlier in a chance meeting, was someone I really would like to get to know better.

We had met at a local farm where I was part of a vegetable gardening community. Actually, it was my son who met Rasmus. Rasmus and his youngest son were on a Sunday tour. They met my son and made a short video about the happy goats living at the farm. Then I came along. In my old boots and gardening clothes – not expecting to meet anyone and certainly not *that* someone.

Later I found out that we both felt immediately comfortable in each other's company. We both felt like sharing our real thoughts during the short dialogue rather than chit chatting about the weather. I didn't think more of it because he was a married man, except that I felt very lucky to have met someone for the first time, and feeling so comfortable just being me.

A few weeks later we met again – also by "chance". We had one friend in common. And that one friend was opening her tiny exhibition hall and we had both decided to be there. I asked Rasmus if he would share the video he made of our sons and the goats. And voilà, we were in contact. Still, I had no further follow-up or thoughts about a relationship. But then I noticed (because now we were connected on social media) that he got divorced. Hmmm. Based on experience, I knew that the adjustment needs some time. So once again no further thoughts of him being that special someone.

Two souls, one thought

After almost a year, I could see that Rasmus was getting to a stage where he was finding his feet after the divorce. That made me think that he IS someone I would really like to get to know better. And guess what? He had exactly the same thought! Rasmus pinged me and asked if we should have coffee sometime soon? Ohhh, YES.

On a Saturday morning, in the middle of the laundry and at the end of a busy week we met for coffee at my house. I promised him coffee – but we just talked and talked and talked while we toured the house and almost forgot – the coffee. Of course I had not mentioned that I had dreamed of sharing the house with someone special – nor that I could not expect that anyone would want to live in the house where I had lived with my ex-husband. Much to my surprise, he said during that first visit: "I can really feel that it is YOU who lives in this house."

I was speechless – because I had not said anything that could lead to reflections of that kind. The manifestations of self love energy in the house and my intentions gave it away. Therefore, as it turned out, he did not have any hesitations about sharing the house with us because the energy was ours and belonged to the present and the future, not the past.

Self love – inside and out

The journey of self love is a never ending story and I am so grateful for that. I am grateful for knowing what it feels like to be comfortable in my own skin. I am loving simply being me. It is no longer something I take for granted.

I fall in and out of varying degrees of self love – and I know that is also part of life and it gives me many new opportunities to learn and grow and to love, not only me but also to share my love with others. When I am authentic and share my self love journey I am also able to love others at an even deeper level and in that way extend the permission for them to also be more of who they really are.

The colors and intentional design and efforts put into my physical surroundings are one of the magic ingredients sprinkled on top of my self love journey. I keep reminding myself that the journey of self love does not have to be super difficult or challenging. Nor does it have to be a lonely ride or one that you must accomplish on our own behind the four walls of home.

I was alone with my son for 5 years, yet not lonely. I felt myself becoming more of who I am – in the amazing company of the participants I met during the personal development program, and with my friends and family. And yesssss, I felt a deepening love for myself that helped me be present in my life with my son. A self love journey that opened the doors for me to meet Rasmus and find a deeper love and relationship than I could ever have imagined.

A big surprise is that the self love journey has also blown the doors to my creativity wide open. Unleashing creativity keeps boosting my feeling of self love and the inner dream team of my creativity indulge in all the colors, shapes and textures of feeling free to be. This creative space is also something I share with Rasmus. Imagine the depth and the dimensions this adds to our relationship and the many levels we connect on.

For me the self love journey has been an opening of my heart to myself and to the love in my life. I'm off to exploring just 'how heart can it be?' both in my private life, in love and in my work-life.

I hope you will also invite creativity along and continuously discover new nuances of self love and feel safe to share the unique colors of your beautiful heart with amazing souls you meet on your way.

About the Author

Lene's love-filled journey is about making an awesome living – just by being herself.

With a background in Learning and Development, Lene enjoys clarifying learning needs, coaching, mentoring, training, and ensuring that employee on-boarding and training design produce excellent results.

As an empath in the corporate world, Lene has found it challenging to follow her heart – until she reframed the situation from "How hard can it be?" to a far more empowering question… "How HEART can it be?"

Fuelled by self-love, Lene is now learning many new skills and experiencing breakthroughs – resulting in her rapidly emerging as a notebook designer, graphic facilitator, a HEARTist. This life-enhancing new emergence is the outcome of uncovering her self-love and embracing her powerful listening skills.

She finds joy in helping others so they can unlock their unique talents, listen to their hearts, and live a life full of joy and purpose.

Connect with Lene through your heart and via www.howheartcanitbe.com

Time

Have you filled your schedule with work, family responsibilities or other activities that would make it difficult to build a healthy relationship? It may be tempting to say that you'll make time when the right person comes along, but I invite you to recognize that your entire energy and attitude may be less than inviting to a potential partner. As you learned, having a vision is important for you as you decide to manifest your relationship. So bear in mind that your potential partner may look at you to see if you fit their vision, too. If you appear to be always busy, running here and there, always saying yes to others while not having much time to yourself, then a potential partner may conclude that you don't fit their ideal.

As Lee-Anne learned, after a painful breakup she needed to spend time alone to heal her disappointment. Then, like Abbey in Chapter 1, Lee used her time to 'date herself' and explore the world — instead of putting off travel and adventure for when the relationship of her dreams would arrive.

The time we create for our self-development is a vital part of the process of manifesting love. And being willing to engage in the activities and outings that you'd ultimately like to experience with your beloved can prime your body and mind for the upcoming reality you'll enjoy with them.

On Manifesting Self-Love

By Lee-Anne Wine

Summer (7 years ago)

It had been a rough year. I was at the point where my heart was physically hurting, tied closely to the emotional trauma that I had experienced. For far too long, the logical side of my brain had been battling the emotions that were constantly threatening to take over. I was only 27 years old with my whole life ahead of me, but I felt like a part of me had died with the disappointments that I had faced within a short period of time.

I had been under the naive impression that if you worked hard and set up your circumstances ideally, the rest would fall into place. I had little thought or consideration for what would happen should my vision fall apart. On a fairly regular basis, I was reviewing my timelines for when I would complete my graduate program, find a job, and get married. I was pleased with myself for the "progress" that I was making in life, but I always felt that there was a piece missing; that there was an unexplainable void that my intuition was constantly trying to push to the surface of my consciousness.

Later, I came to find out that what I was missing from my storyline was a deep love for myself, and that it was this love that required cultivating and exploring. Sometimes the universe will present you with a perfect opportunity to enrich your life, and for too long, I had been ignoring those signs since they did not fit into my life model at the time. It was only when a part of my perfect plan came to a halt that my world view was challenged. Here is that part of my story.

As it turned out, the boyfriend that I planned to marry disclosed to me, after four years of being together, that he had cheated on me. Upon hearing the news, I was confused and in disbelief. In a reaction purely based on the shock to my system, I tried to negotiate with him that in fact it was not true and that he had not cheated on me. (This is what shock and grief will do; I was in denial and bargaining at the same time). When he continued to explain the circumstances to me, I knew deep inside that without question, my world as I knew it had changed. I later came to understand that what had felt like the worst possible heartache, had become one of my biggest life lessons.

If I had been honest with myself, I would have come to understand and recognize sooner, the immense amount of social pressure that I had been feeling to meet particular timelines. I was feeling so rushed by life that I was simply going along for the ride and trying to tick off as many boxes as I could. In hindsight, I realize how very unhealthy this approach to life was, but at the same time, I look around me and see so many people adhering to the same timelines and expectations on a daily basis. The problem is societal and it interferes directly with our personal growth, our life journeys and our happiness.

While packing my bags in preparation to return to my childhood home, I let my feelings of heartache, fear, sadness, abandonment and shame move through my body. It had been months since my boyfriend had told me that he cheated, and although we tried to give our relationship a chance, I knew that in the long run it would not work out for the best. It became apparent that we shared different values from the outset. I knew I had to start over, and that a renewal would bring dramatic changes to the way I approached life, love, and relationships, because I was determined not to find myself in that situation again.

That first night home, I lay in my childhood bed waiting for the heartbreak and tears to wash over me. Those first few tears were quick to come, since I had been trying to keep myself composed for most of the day. I was fully prepared to allow for the pain to lull me to sleep, as it had done now for many months. But this time was noticeably different. The tears did not accompany a deep pain in my chest, nor did I ruminate over the list of questions in my head as to why this happened to me, and what I could have done differently. Instead, for the first time, in the depths of silence, I realized that these were tears of acceptance, of understanding and of peace. I felt the strong pull of my intuition – my inner guide – soothing me and replacing deep-seated feelings of fear with feelings of renewal and freedom. The dread that I had felt about having to start over was replaced with the excitement of getting to start over.

My perspective had dramatically shifted; I was filled with energy and drive to get out into the world and discover what I was made of and what I wanted from this lifetime. I had been on the trajectory of fulfilling societal expectations for so long that I was curious to see what life could look like outside of the prescribed norms. I drifted off to sleep that night knowing that a seed had been planted, and that my intuition would guide me on my journey as long as I was willing to follow the signs along the way.

I woke up early that next morning and instinctively knew I wanted more from life. Rather than feeling exhausted, depleted, and broken, I was feeling energized and hopeful. I sat down with my coffee and my journal ready to begin exploring new opportunities. Before my pen could hit paper, I heard one word pop into my head — TRAVEL.

I have always been a traveler, and have always felt a sense of relief and solace in stepping off of a plane in a foreign land. It feels as if you're leaving all of life's problems behind. I was craving this relief and looking for a new life adventure. My heart told me that this was a journey I needed to take alone. Before I had the opportunity to find excuses or talk myself out of it, I purchased a non-refundable ticket to Southeast Asia that was scheduled to depart in only a few weeks' time. I made the commitment to listen to my inner voice and I was determined to follow through.

Manifesting Love

In early August, I packed a backpack with a few essential items and boarded a plane to Southeast Asia en route to Ho Chi Minh (Saigon City). I had no idea what the adventure ahead looked like, but I was overwhelmed by every emotion in the book. I had never travelled so far on my own, and I was worried about being able to navigate an entirely new culture in a place where I did not speak the language or know the customs.

As the plane took off, I was cursing myself for having not even purchased a traveller's guide to where I was headed. I quickly discovered that there was not one single passenger around me who spoke English fluently, and I felt alone and scared. I closed my eyes, I focused on my breath, and I willed for that sensation of comfort to envelope me and let me know I was on the right path. After several long minutes, no such sensation came. I felt very alone and abandoned by my inner guide.

After more than twenty hours of travelling, several stopovers, naps on airport floors, and desperate attempts at finding decent coffee, I arrived at my hotel in the city. It was 11:30 p.m. local time and I was hungry, tired and disoriented. I decided to crawl into bed and start fresh the next day.

Following a long night of tossing and turning, I reluctantly dragged myself out of bed the next morning and decided to hit the streets. I was in desperate need of coffee and I could not tell the difference between what was someone's home or a business. Everything looked the same, and I found myself wandering into local's homes asking about nearby restaurants.

After a few more minutes of walking I could see Starbucks across a large intersection. I am usually not a huge advocate of going to Starbucks in a foreign country where I like to immerse myself in the local culture, but with my strong desire for caffeine, paired with a feeling of relief upon seeking something familiar from home, I caved. I had one problem ... I honestly did not know how to cross the intersection safely without traffic lights, and with hundreds of mopeds moving at different paces in different directions.

I had been warned about crossing the streets in Saigon, but I had no idea what that meant until that moment. I bravely stepped out into traffic and was just nearly missed by a moped, followed by honking and yelling. At that moment, another tourist from New Zealand offered to take my hand and show me the ropes, leading me safely to my destination across the street. It was a small but powerful gesture, as I was reminded that I needed to lean on others from time to time, and that this journey would require me to take chances and live in the moment.

As I became more comfortable moving through the city streets, and with the support of friends that I had met along the way, I travelled from the South to the North learning about culture, food, history, landscape, weather patterns and most importantly, myself. Long journeys on overnight trains riddled with cockroaches and dirty beds reminded me of the comforts that I had left behind at home. Long days transversing urban terrain and countryside reminded me of the vastness of the world in which we live, and it left me wanting more.

I felt liberated as I made my way through the days on my schedule and at my own pace. I stopped scanning menu items for familiar foods, instead embracing whatever was put on my plate. This ranged from endless variations of noodles to deep fried tarantulas and fire ants. Every day brought with it a new adventure and a new insight into better understanding myself.

Being out in the world on my own taught me to go with the flow; to have reasonable expectations, and to be pleasantly surprised. The vastness of the landscapes humbled and grounded me. The poverty I observed first-hand filled me with both heartbreak and gratitude. Traveling as a single female meant that I always had to have one eye open and be well aware of my surroundings. I had to build up my relationship with my intuition, and relied heavily on this mind-body connection because in some formidable circumstances, it made the difference between life and death. I learned that things are not always as they appear, and that the grass is not always greener. I came to understand that you can plan all you want, but sometimes the unanticipated obstacles along the way are responsible for the most pivotal moments in our lives.

Learning to love and trust yourself will help you to discover, adapt, and have the courage to go for everything you could possibly want in life. And, if those things do not work out as you had planned and hoped, well, then that is okay, too. I learned to put myself out there, and to be open to the possibilities. Most importantly, I learned to love me, and knew that l was returning home a changed person.

I had forgotten how to love myself. It had not been factored into my "perfect" life plan because I was so caught up in what I thought my life should look like, and the path I would follow. I was so focused on adhering to the timeline that society dictates, that I never once stopped to really and truly consider what I wanted out of MY life. Without having had my heart broken, I would never have had the opportunity to make it whole.

As the plane touched down on the tarmac in my hometown, Toronto, I had no idea what the future held, and the thought of that thrilled me. I knew this was an opportunity to rebuild and rediscover what it was that I truly wanted and needed from life. I cannot honestly say that the pain in my heart had completely subsided, but I know that without that painful detour, I might never have had the opportunity to discover all that I love about myself. With this profound love, I continue to change the lives of those around me, always challenging others to consider a different perspective, dive deeper into the barometer of their emotions, and know that whatever they want in life is worth pursuing.

A mere three months later, I buckled up my seatbelt as the captain announced our descent into the beautiful landscape of South America. I looked out the window as I waited for the plane to dip below the clouds, and contemplated what this next chapter of my life would look like. I packed my journal back into my carry-on, and sat back in my seat to close my eyes and take in the moment. With that old familiar mix of fear and anticipation, I was ready for my next adventure.

About the Author

Lee-Anne Wine is a Toronto-based therapist and yoga teacher, working with clients on issues related to anxiety, depression, and life transitions in a multitude of settings. Her journey began over a decade ago, when with passion and a non-judgmental approach, Lee got involved in the homeless community in Toronto, digging into the systemic barriers and challenges that she recognized along the way. Her later work involved working in the frontline trenches of the child protection system in Canada to support some of the country's most vulnerable people.

Lee spends most of her days committed to personal development and helping her clients cultivate a healthy work/life balance, feel grounded in themselves and cultivate self-growth with practical tools and skills along the way.

In her spare time, Lee can always be found walking in nature, journaling, doing yoga and listening to music!

Get in touch with Lee online at www.Leeannewine.com or on Instagram; @changeyourbrain

Surrender in Faith

As Karan and Eric discovered, there comes a moment in our pursuit of a new partner that we must surrender, let go of the striving, and let the Universe work its magic.

In the case of Ofkje Teekens, she went through several refusals to accept the love that was offered to her! And Karena Virginia also found herself shying away from meeting the man who would become her husband. Ultimately, both Ofkje and Karena had to surrender, face their fears and trust in the divine. They have now been happily married for 30 and 20 years, respectively. While their stories did not any manifesting rituals, they illustrate an important lesson in having faith in the process, and yourself.

This Love Story Was Meant to Be

By Ofkje Teekens

September 1985. It has been 35 years!

I was a young woman of 25, at university and close to graduation. I can say I was quite pretty and I'd had some boyfriends, who were all called Rob or Robert.

But after a few Roberts, suddenly there was Kees. A different name, and for me really special. He later told me he was normally very shy, but not at that time. He told his mum about me and she said, "If you know for sure, go for it!"

And he did. After all these years I'm still happy he was so persistent.

But I was resistant.

I also talked about my 'boyfriend' with my mum. I had nearly finished my studies but had missed a few exams being busy with 'boyfriends'. It was just that I didn't know what I wanted. Yes, of course, I wanted to have a boyfriend. But I also appreciated my freedom – and that was a conflict.

I listened to the advice of my mother who said, "First of all, finish your studies. If he's the right one, he will wait." I had to laugh, but I knew she was right. And he did wait, persistently and full of patience!

I appreciated that he waited. He was a nice man, five years older than me. He had read a lot of books and he knew about many things — and I really liked that. He was a funny guy and he was really interested in me, interested in what I thought and what I did. And that was quite new for me.

I came from a big family. I had four 'mothers': my own mother and three older sisters. They knew everything better. At least, better than me and my two younger twin brothers. So Prince Kees made me very happy. He paid me a lot of attention and I really liked that. We talked a lot, which was very special, because normally he doesn't talk much. He is more about watching and observing.

Our meeting seemed pure coincidence. It was in the bookstore where I worked to earn money to pay for my university studies. The store was one of the biggest in the Netherlands, in Utrecht. At that time, 34 years ago, around 2,000 customers a day frequented the store.

My first duty was to help sell the books. Dutch literature, crime, poetry. It was a good parallel with my study of Dutch language and Literature.

I loved my work and enjoyed meeting and greeting people and I loved to help them find the right book. After some time I had my own regular customers, and when they came in we had excellent conversations.

At that time, I also taught literature courses. And it happened that I needed only one more client to complete my course.

This is how I met my Prince.

Every afternoon I started working at 1pm.

On 9th September, there he was, in the bookstore at 1:08pm. This is where it all starts, the story of my heart. He opened it with patience.

Was it fate? For had he been there ten minutes earlier, we would never have met!

He asked me a normal question, the kind customers often ask. He was kind but at that moment I wasn't impressed. It certainly wasn't love at first sight.

I helped him to find the book he wanted. He looked happy and gave me a newspaper that contained his first publication. I thanked him. Looking back, for him it must have been very scary to talk to me in the first place.

But for me it was business as usual.

I had been polite and kind but I had a lot of other customers in the bookstore.

That morning I had already been given a pie, a newspaper and now this customer had given me his first published article.

So, it was nothing special. I carried on working in the bookstore in the afternoons and on Thursday evenings and all day on Saturdays.

Despite all the people I met at my work, I felt a bit lost. I was living alone, taking care of myself. I was nearly at the end of my studies and in a few months I would graduate. What would the future hold?

After my exams, I was hoping to become a teacher at a school for teenagers. But in those days, there were few jobs available in education.

I forgot about my Prince, but he did not forget me... !

At that time I also had another job, teaching at the adult university, I loved it, enjoying working with people, helping and serving them. The manager there told me that a young man named Kees had called several times, asking for me. I didn't remember him so I was wondering who he was.

He left his number so I called it, wondering who on earth this person could be.

He explained he wanted more information about my courses. He couldn't come to my information evening and would love to make an appointment. I was curious about this. I felt something I had never felt before! The following Saturday he picked me up after work to go for a drink so that I could answer his questions. But there were no questions at all!

He just wanted to meet me again. What was he up to? I got a bit nervous and felt misled. I wanted to leave the restaurant but something made me stay. I was surprised and I suppose a bit flattered. I did not expect us to spend the whole afternoon together. He invited me for dinner, but that was too much. He was a bit disappointed and said in that case he had to eat an omelet with his mum.

It was remarkable that I walked with him all the way to the train station. Why did I do that? Because I didn't want to see him again, did I? There were some questions for me to answer about my feelings. But I pushed my feelings away. I was a bit confused to say the least!

I noticed that I felt a bit scared by all the attention I was receiving from this man I did not know at all. After seeing him constantly bringing me flowers, one of my colleagues asked if I was in love. I said I didn't think so. To be honest, I was confused. Was I in love?

At the end of that week I told my colleague that I would give this man a call to stop all of this. I had no time for men at the moment, I needed to study. But I felt reluctant! What did this man want from me? I couldn't even remember his face. Could I cancel that last date?

How to get rid of my Prince?

So after work, I phoned him to say that I didn't want to see him again. He was full of patience again, and he seemed to understand. He was so kind. Could I trust him? Did I want to trust anybody anymore, after those other boys with their smooth talk? But he was very entertaining and the phone call lasted for hours.

After a couple of hours I got tired and needed to use the bathroom. "No worries," he said. "Just give me your telephone number and I will call you back in ten minutes."

How stupid was I? I did.

I remember my face in the bathroom mirror and how excited I felt. What was going on? Was he the man I was looking for? That evening was the beginning of meeting my Prince on a deeper level. That evening I met him in my soul.

He called me back a few times that evening. Full of energy and persistence.

We had wonderful conversations about all kinds of things! What was going on?

Back then, there was no such thing as FaceTime. So, what did he look like? I couldn't remember. I had lost the memory. I got lost that evening.

In the upcoming weeks we spoke a lot on the telephone. We didn't see each other because I had to pass my exams. He entertained me then let me be so I could concentrate.

After a few weeks I finished my exams and I was so proud of myself! It had been hard for me to do my studies. Ten years later I understood why. My son has dyslexia and after a test I found out that I have dyslexia, too.

The Prince meets his Princess!

I finished my studies and he invited me to come to The Hague, a beautiful royal city near the sea. I agreed to visit him. He wanted to meet me at the train station but I resisted again and I told him I would find my own way. I really was a little nervous as I travelled to his place.

When I arrived upstairs I realized that again I couldn't remember his face. I only remembered his voice, so kind and full of patience. Full of love. He stood in the door opening, with a smile on his face. He took me in his arms and held me. Then he kissed me. At that moment I knew it! He was the one. I could feel it in my heart.

We had a wonderful afternoon. We talked a lot again, as if we hadn't spoken to anyone for months. Were we soulmates who had found each other? I couldn't believe it.

We went to the beach and had a romantic walk hand in hand along the seaside. And then one moment he stopped and kissed me, a very long kiss. We didn't see the wave coming, and our shoes got totally soaked. A circle of people were around us, clapping their hands. We had a big laugh together.

All of this was so special, the sea and the water. At that moment, I felt no resistance at all. But it soon returned. I felt insecure again. Could I trust him? He asked me to stay for the night, but I feared an intimate connection. I didn't stay over.

Life went on but I felt different. We were connected. He came over from the Hague to have a wonderful dinner that I cooked for him. I felt totally at ease with him and we met and talked a lot. We took several walks and on the weekends we stayed together at my place.

After my graduation, he bought me my first golden ring and I was so happy. I still couldn't believe he liked me and loved me. I felt so grateful.

I still worked in the bookshop. A beautiful flower shop opened nearby and he bought a rose for me. From that moment on, he had the florist send me beautiful flowers every month. He stole my heart!

The persistence of the Prince and the resistance of the Princess

Then the Prince asked me to move into his castle.

My mother taught me to take good care of myself. Be independent and earn your own money! But my Prince persisted with patience and gave me some time to get used to the idea. I said I would only move once I'd found a job there. After all those years on my own, was there space enough in my heart to live with somebody?

I wanted to live with him. But I was afraid to share my heart, my life. I was afraid of being vulnerable.

I had become so used to protecting myself. To being prepared. But what was I protecting myself from? And what was I preparing myself for? Could I trust him? Was I good enough? Did I have enough self-compassion to let me love and accept myself? But he was so persistent!

The Prince came to rescue me from my struggle. And again he did so in a creative and romantic way. This time he made a special little book. It was his invitation for me to stop hiding.

The special little book that he made for me was entitled "The Burglary".

When I opened it, I saw a mirror in the book. No story. He made it for me so that when I was reading this 'book' I could always look in the mirror to check if there was somebody behind me. So that I could feel confident. I started laughing. All that effort, only for me. I felt so thrilled. He made my heart sing, this Prince!

The Princess moved to the Prince's castle

After three months I moved to be with my Prince and began living in the royal city, The Hague. I found a job there at an educational publisher. Earning my own money gave me a good feeling.

A month later he gave me another spectacular surprise. A poem.

It looked very structured. There were nice words about love within the rhyme. But there was something else . He told me to read the first letter of each sentence. And to build a sentence out of these letters. It said:

WILL YOU MARRY ME?

I felt like a queen! I had no doubts anymore. I wanted to drop that resistance, and I did. I felt the transition of love. I could really embrace his love for the first time. I felt surrender.

The King and Queen build their own castle together!

On 8th May 1987 we got married in a castle in Voorburg on a beautiful sunny day. We've now been married for 33 years.

Two children were born at the castle. A Prince and a Princess.

We have a lovely and happy family. My son, the Prince, has married his Princess and I'm the proud grandmother of a lovely grandson.

The circle is complete for now.

I chose to write and share this very personal story to help and serve other people. If you've ever wondered does love really exist, you now know it does! Yessss! You may say yes to the dress!

Love does exist, but only when you can open your heart. You can meet your 'lover' anywhere. In my case it was in a bookstore. Do you want to manifest love? For me it was all about self-love. Be your authentic self and you will shine!

Your Prince or Princess will show up!

With Love,
Ofkje Teekens

About the Author

Ofkje Teekens (1960) is a Dutch Jungian psychologist, a transformational teacher, an author and an international speaker. After a successful career in education for more than 25 years, including running her own institute for children with learning disorders, she switched to coaching.

Ofkje has created several games for personal growth and coaching (Young Talent, Life-Shift, Life-Blossom and Life-Web) and many card decks on actual themes like Burn Out, Self-Compassion, Archetypes & Talents and Blooming Mindset. She also co-created a card deck about Money Archetypes and a card deck called Masquerade. She developed an online Archetype Quest training program, a training for Life-Shift and co-developed an online program for a Blooming Mindset.

Ofkje has written several books, the latest are on Life-Shift. In 2020 she hosted 24 shows on Awake TV Network and created the Facebook Community Blooming Women Society.

Connect with Ofkje online:
www.ofkjeteekens.com/en
https://www.facebook.com/ofkje.teekens
https://www.facebook.com/groups/271094520701905/

I Knew I Loved You Before I Met You

By Karena Virginia

Souls find one another when the time is aligned between two hearts and God's unwavering love. I know this to be true from the depths of my heart, and writing this now is my gift of hope for all who read it. I knew I loved my husband before I even met him, and when our eyes met, it was confirmation that my prayers were heard, answered and delivered. Do you believe in miracles?

Living in New York City was challenging for me. As a highly sensitive person, the crowds and noise felt contracting, sticky and loud. I think the loneliest time in my life was the time I spent in the city with the most people. Being around thousands of people and feeling alone and different can make a person second guess themselves. *Is there something wrong with me? Am I supposed to go to the bar and have a beer when all I want to do is get under a blanket with a good book? Is staying home because my soul wants to be home a waste of my life? Perhaps I need to push myself and show up with friends?*

So I did. Going out on dates with strangers felt like a string of Saturday night job interviews. Who wants to be on a job interview when they have two baby nephews who would love to cuddle their auntie? I wanted to be a mommy. All I wanted was to raise children. I wanted out of the city where the men took me to nice restaurants and expected something in return and then said goodbye with disappointment. Over and over again. Sometimes they pushed and I felt like a piece of meat after being naively open hearted and loving while having wine and dinner. Were my fun loving humor and my thoughts on life not valuable? Were there any men in New York City who wanted what I wanted?

That is when I left the city. That is when I left my career as an actress too. I stopped going to LA, and I said goodbye to my agent. It was my yoga and meditation practice that gave me the courage to follow my heart when my friends and family thought I was making a huge mistake.

Following the heart is the gift of life. The heart is the north star, and the divine speaks to us through the heart. Imagine the miracle of the heart that started beating inside the womb way before our brains were developed. The heart IS the miracle.

Life in the countryside

I moved into the country. My little house was so cozy. There were candles, a fireplace, a bathtub and a refrigerator which I filled with healthy food. I did not drink or party. I meditated and juiced instead. I did not have a television. I read books instead. I had the best stereo and I played soft music or mantra throughout the day and night. I wrote in my journal. I practiced the law of attraction way before it was a trendy phrase.

I started a yoga teachers' training program a bit north of where I was. The school was called Yoga Mountain and it was far into the mountains. Further from where a single woman who wants to have babies and get married should be. It was beautiful, and it was weird to most. Yoga was weird to most at that time anyway. However, my heart felt happy. I sensed the miracles because I felt myself making space for them. I spent my Saturday nights with my nephews.

Sometimes there was a deep sadness inside of me as if part of me was missing. A void or emptiness in my stomach. Like a part of me was not there. I feared that I would never feel complete, and reminded myself that being complete was about finding comfort in being alone with myself. Friends were having babies, and my sister was in the Miss America pageant. I had given up my career, and I felt quite lost.

A helping hand

Trust your heart, I would hear in my dreams. One day I booked a modeling job in New York City, and felt a depression that took over my body. It was hard to even get out of bed that day. My body was bloated and my period was absent. Something shut down inside of me, and energy was stuck. I knew it. Maybe it had been a mistake to move into the middle of nowhere.

I got on my knees and I prayed to God to please give me hope. Looking back I realize that I was dealing with a chemical and hormonal depression, and it makes sense now how helpless I felt. Somehow making it to the city, I put on the outfit that was now too tight, and began doing the work.

On the modeling assignment with me was Claudia, a stunning Australian. I remembered her from other jobs, but she was too beautiful to talk to. She was stunning. I imagined that she had a perfect life. I was feeling so sad, and covering up my feelings has never been my way. Fortunately, we were assigned as partners by the client. I needed her hand.

"Trust in the Lord with all your heart, and lean not on your own understanding, but in all your ways acknowledge Him, and He will make straight your paths." Claudia taught me that bible verse, and said her grandmother reminded her of it consistently. It became my mantra and Claudia became my friend. We began studying the bible together and with flowering essences and herbs and beautiful healers, my period returned along with my hope.

Matchmaking in NYC

In December of 1999 I went to a Christmas party and sat with a coworker and her husband. I was my goofy self, having fun and speaking authentically about life. The bar was hopping, and enjoying a single glass of wine was the extent of my evening out partying. I used to leave parties early, and always liked to be in bed by 10. Quite boring, I know. And not the prescription for meeting a man, but I had to be me. So I left.

The next morning my coworker called me and said that her husband thought I should meet his friend, Chuck Virginia. "He is a lawyer. He is picky. He lives in New York City," she said. I was polite, and said I would think about it. But quietly I felt a feeling of 'no way'. Not a NYC guy. Not a lawyer. And definitely not someone picky who would think I was a yogi weirdo. What was her husband thinking?

Months went by, and I was feeling lonely. I wondered if I would ever meet someone who would melt my heart. I was too picky myself. I decided to give it a go when my friend Katie said, "I don't know, Karena—I think you and Chuck are a great match." So, we set up a blind date with Chuck Virginia. He was driving to New Jersey on a Friday to play golf, and then the four of us were to meet at a restaurant. But then I cancelled. Left them with a message to tell Chuck on the golf course that I changed my mind. He was picky, and he was probably just like the NYC guys I had dated the year before, when I lived there. I was feeling sensitive and vulnerable, and I was frightened of being rejected for being me. Not going.

I spent that summer in a deeply spiritual place that was so healing. Continuing my yoga and meditation practice along with journaling was comforting. I trusted God so deeply, and I remembered my new mantra daily:

"Trust in the Lord with all your heart, and lean not on your own understanding, but in all your ways acknowledge Him, and He will make straight your paths."

Hiking in nature was beautiful. Spending time with my nephews warmed my heart. Reading books was cozy, and listening to soft music always brought me a sense of peace. I prayed often, and spent time with married friends and their kids. Taking a bath at night and sleeping early was my ritual. Friends went out to bars, and I stayed in with my coziness.

I knew it was time

A few of us at work won a trip to Bermuda. Stephanie, my little sister, was my date. We had so much fun riding through the small streets on a scooter and watching the sun rise and set daily. Since I was a scooter spaz at the rentals, my sister drove it and I sat on the back. We laughed at the fact that they would not give me one of my own. Katie and her husband laughed, and I laughed with them. My sister sang one evening at the celebration event, and everyone was blown away by her talent. She is a magical, magnetic and radiantly talented woman. She won the talent award in the Miss America pageant just a year before, and she inspired us all. I have always been so proud of her.

The next morning my sister and I went to church in Bermuda. We drove our little scooter in our pink and green dresses. Like little girls in a way. We met a beautiful couple outside the church who we spoke to for a while, and I said, "My dream is to find a partner who looks at me in front of the church the same way that the two of you are looking at each other right now."

I felt something come over me in that moment. It was as if God was informing my heart that it was time to truly love myself enough to meet my soulmate. It felt like a knowing and also a call for bravery against my fear of rejection. Somehow in that moment, as the Bermuda sun was shining upon me, and beautiful pink flowers bloomed in my peripheral vision, I knew it was time.

When we arrived home, Katie called me and said, "Al does not say much, Karena, but he will not stop talking about how you must meet his childhood friend, Chuck Virginia."

Even hearing his name again did something to me. *Virginia as a last name? Chuck? Maybe he is Charles but they call him Chuck in his family?* I still don't know why the name Chuck did something to me, but I remembered that light outside the church in Bermuda and said, "Yes."

On Friday, Aug 28th 1999, I drove down the Garden State parkway wearing a lavender sweater with a soft furry collar, bare legs with a black skirt which went to my knees, and black sandals. I was listening to *Anatomy of the Spirit* on tape. To this day, that is one of my favorite books. I will always be so grateful for the vessel Carolyn Myss is for spirit.

As I drove with the sun beginning to set above me, I heard Carolyn's voice remind me of Grace. *What is Grace? Grace is this moment, I thought. Grace is the miracle that God is creating and each mile I drive is bringing me closer.* I felt it all.

*"I knew I loved you before I met you.
I think I dreamed you into life.
I knew I loved you before I met you.
I have been waiting all my life."*

~ Savage Garden 1999

God wants this for me

We met. I saw his green eyes. I recognized him. I loved him. I knew him. I wanted him in my arms like I have never wanted anything. I gasped. My soul began longing as if I had lost him in another life and had found him again at that moment. My heart was beating outside my chest.

He was so calm. So relaxed. So smooth. So precious.

I was petrified. How was it possible to fall in love so quickly? How could I be so vulnerable?

We went to the restaurant and I sat next to him. I kept catching my breath. *God loves me. God wants this for me. I have faith. I trust. I know this is the answer to my prayer.* This was my internal monologue, an attempt to calm my nerves.

I went to the bathroom and called my mom to tell her I had just met my husband.

This is all divine

The Friday night after we met, I tossed and turned all night long. My eyes were closed, but my heartbeat was too strong for sleep. I was so deeply in love.

He did not call until Tuesday, and on Sunday and Monday night ironically I was ok. My mind was filled with so many thoughts... *He is a smooth operator. He knows. This is all divine. God knows. How can I love this deeply this fast and have him not care?*

We went out for dinner Friday night and again I could hardly eat. We kissed for the first time after dinner in my country home. He left. I was up all night again.

On Monday I saw my spiritual therapist, Kathy, and I shared my fear with her.

"What if he doesn't feel the same way?" I asked.

"Then it is not meant to be," she reminded me.

"But it is," I said.

"Then trust," she said.

Later I found out that he was having the same conversation with his therapist, Stacy, in New York City. We told each other. We laughed.

Three weeks later, in the middle of September, I joined him on his business trip to Sedona, Arizona. While he was in a meeting, I went to the vortexes and did a ritual of gratitude for his presence in my life. I felt subtle healing energy and a tingling on my skin. Love overtook every cell in my body and my heart opened bigger than the sky above me. Everything appeared miraculous. My soul was awakening.

On December 5th, 2019, Charles Raymond Virginia asked me to be his wife. That evening we were intimate for the first time, and it was the most beautiful exchange of energy I had ever experienced in my life.

Six months later on June 20th, we celebrated our marriage with family and friends. Charles is my sunshine—he has been my sunshine since that light shined upon me in front of that miraculous church in Bermuda.

Love is ready for you. Trusting the divine and opening your heart is the path to the miracle. May love find you as love found me. We are all children of the same God who loves us unconditionally.

Charles and I have been married for twenty years as I write this in August 2020, and I will finish this with a letter Charles wrote to me for our anniversary.

Dear Karena,

You are more than a wife, a lover, a best friend to me. You are all those things, but in addition, you are to me something ephemeral. An idea. You have been this to me since I first became conscious of romantic love as a young boy. The idea of being made whole by someone, the filling of that void we have until we find our soulmate. It takes growing on one's own to make it possible for this type of alchemy to happen. We did that. You are a dream come true for me. I had to do a lot of work to make you possible. And I had to wait a long time. But you appeared.

Our wedding song says it all [song above by Savage Garden]. You are the embodiment of the wish. I have always felt like the luckiest guy in the world because of you. There is not a day that I don't pinch myself that I am with you. And one of the greatest things about this is knowing that it will never change. It is everlasting love. Eternal.

About the Author

Karena Virginia is an inspirational speaker and healer who brings deep spiritual mysticism to the modern world in a cozy and embracing style. Karena shares kundalini yoga and spiritual practices to heal the trauma that resides in our energy bodies and allow the love from our hearts to shine forth so we can live a life of fulfillment, happiness, and health.

Karena is a member of Oprah Winfrey's Belief team, and her passion is to bring the technology of ancient and miraculous healing to the masses as seen in her highly acclaimed yoga video, "The Power of Kundalini Yoga," the popular "Relax and Attract" App and her latest book, *Essential Kundalini Yoga*, which is bringing light and transformation into the hearts of many people around the world.

Connect with Karena online at www.KarenaVirginia.com

Chapter 5
Create Your Own Manifesting Process

As you learned from the stories presented already in this book, you may not need any formal process to manifest your soul-aligned relationship. But if you want to be a deliberate, conscious co-creator of the next chapter in your life it can be helpful to engage in a ritual or ceremony, as the next story illustrates.

Margaretha had been doing deep healing and discovery work on herself, including taking time off from dating, before formally making a declaration to the Universe of her readiness to manifest love. The ceremony that she created one evening was clearly magical. It has led to a beautiful love story that lives on in amazing harmony and growth.

After reading her story it's up to you to make your bold declaration to the Universe, say a prayer asking for your soulmate to arrive, or meditate to connect directly with your beloved in a soul connection. Write a letter to your beloved telling them what you are excited to share in the near future. In your daily meditations, imagine holding hands or doing other activities in your vision from Chapter 4.

Manifesting the Love of My Life at 35

By Margaretha Tosi

For years I had a tough relationship with anger and rage. One that I was ashamed of more than anything else. I hid it the best that I could for as long as I could, always pushing those dark feelings away as soon as they built up. As long as I was pushing and laughing them away I thought they couldn't hurt me, but I've never been so wrong. Keeping up my appearance and pretending everything was fine kept me 'safe', until that spring day in April 2004.

I was in my mid-twenties, at home in the Netherlands. The sun was shining through the windows, spreading light and warmth into the living room. I opened the garden door and breathed in the lovely spring air. Energised, I turned on some music and started my morning chores. While vacuuming, I began to feel frustrated and angry. I knew those feelings very well but always kept them inside, afraid of what might happen if I let them out. At that moment, the vacuum cleaner didn't move how I wanted it to and I snapped. All the built-up frustration, anger, hurt and disappointment, mostly towards myself, came to the surface and I blacked out.

Coming to my senses a few minutes later, I looked at the vacuum cleaner cord in amazement. In my rage, I had yanked it so hard from the socket that I had taken off a part of the concrete wall. That's when it hit me that my rage and frustration were completely out of proportion. I needed to take action. But how? Where? And who could I turn to?

Feeling ashamed of my emotions, especially my rage, I closed myself up again. I hid behind the wall of 'I'm fine' to keep functioning, and kept on doing my chores. I knew exactly what I was doing; I just didn't have the courage or the tools to deal with it or talk about it. There were smaller occurrences that had built up towards this huge blackout, but again, I kept them all inside of myself.

That afternoon 'coincidently' my mum came to visit and saw the hole in the wall. I was so worried that she would be angry with me that I broke down. I cried so hard that I could barely speak. I was finally able to tell her how confused I felt, but I couldn't find the right words to explain what was going on. The only thing I knew was that I couldn't continue living that way. I was so grateful when my mum held me, softly shushed me and told me it was okay. 'I've seen this coming,' she said. 'You've been struggling for quite some time and I didn't know how to reach out to help you.'

I felt so relieved. There was no rejection, no anger, only understanding. After a cup of tea, she handed me a small piece of paper she had found hanging on a bulletin board at a local shop. It had a phone number written on it and two words: 'Surrendering and Struggling'. Even though I wanted to deny that they resonated with me, I knew they rang true. I had been struggling for so long, it was time to surrender.

Those words and that little piece of paper led me to a lovely holistic coach who helped me through some deep-rooted limiting beliefs and behaviours that I was finally able to acknowledge and let go of. Those beliefs included always feeling not good enough, or less than others. Less smart or successful. A quitter for not finishing my training as a psychiatric nurse, giving up 5 months before graduation. I hadn't been able to continue after a patient's suicide had triggered memories of a former boyfriend's suicide attempt. It had all been just too much to handle at the age of 20.

Within half a year of first meeting my coach, I decided that I wanted to support others in the same way. So, I started a holistic coaching education that changed my life. It has brought me closer to myself, allowing me to know myself on a level that I had never experienced before. I learned to trust my instincts and accept all my spirituality with love.

Yet I was still not able to break the bad relationship cycle I'd been in for many years...

Breaking free

I was in the midst of an unhappy relationship that took me 2 more years to break out of. Breaking out of this made me understand that I needed to care for myself first, and love myself enough to break free from a toxic and undesirable situation.

People who know me know that I love cuddles and hugs. And living with someone who froze every time I tried to give or receive this affection hurt me to my core and I felt rejected every time I tried. So I stopped trying and something inside me died.

The aftermath was not pretty and I just wanted to escape from all the difficulties. So that's exactly what I did.

I was working at that time in one of the biggest university hospitals in the Netherlands, managing the trauma department, and that's where I met 'my escape'. He was a man who seemed to have everything I had been missing for the last 9 years. He was warm, cuddly, loved hugs and was always there for me, or so I thought, even though I had a deep instinctive feeling of doubt and mistrust towards him. I had been cheated on before but I decided to ignore my inner wisdom and just go with it. I really wanted this escape to work.

We went travelling, had lovely dinners, and he spoiled me with clothes, jewellery and handbags. A girl's dream come true. I still had those feelings of mistrust tugging at me, but again I ignored my inner wisdom even though I was often sick to my stomach.

I couldn't shake these strong signals from my body, so I started checking his phone and found the most disgusting texts to and from other women who he had obviously been with. When I confronted him he said I was overreacting, and that I was wrong for going through his phone and for not trusting him. I'd got it all wrong, he said. It was not until he stepped it up a notch and became really disrespectful towards me that I realised I'd had enough. I left him because I just couldn't be THAT 'blind' anymore. I was heartbroken and happy at the same time. I took a few belongings and moved out of our apartment.

I decided to take a break from relationships with men and to work on the relationship I had with myself instead. Specifically, the one of being alone with me, myself and I. I bought an apartment and made it mine. There were many times when I just wanted to pick up the phone to my ex and invite him back because I was so lonely. Fortunately, I have a dear bestie, Xaviera, and we've always agreed that if either of us has the urge to call someone who had done us wrong, we would call each other first. And so I did … many times.

Each time, she supported me on my way to healing. Being able to be alone and happy is a gift only I could give myself. The balance and self-love present in my life was just divine and I enjoyed it fully.

In 2012, I was enjoying life in a way that I'd not known before. Being single for 2 years was the best thing I could have ever done for myself. I truly felt I was coming out 'whole' — as me, myself and I.

My manifesting ceremony

I knew I was ready for the right man in my life now, and I knew the universe was listening. After being single and reconnecting with my first biggest love, the Universe, our connection grew stronger and stronger every day. So I knew how I could ask her to join me in a ceremony to manifest the man of my dreams and the love of my life.

So, one evening I sat on my sofa in my small but cosy apartment and a strong but gentle push urged me to create a ceremonial evening, one full of magic and manifestation.

I put on some soul music — the type of music that just moves my whole soul and heart. With the rhythm of the most beautiful song, I lit some candles all around my apartment and in my mosaic bowl. When I switched off the main lights and looked around, my magical space had arrived. I braided my long hair and changed into my most beautiful dress, feeling like a goddess.

I sat down on my sofa and took out a piece of paper. 'Dear Universe,' I wrote, 'I need your guidance and help to find the man I will marry. He needs to be honest, loyal, trustworthy, a family man and a *man*.'

I then sent my lovely list to the Universe, burning the piece of paper and waving the smoke up into the magical air of my apartment. I blew out the candles that had accompanied me throughout the ritual of writing the list of desires and went to bed.

During this time, I had been researching my Italian roots from my father's side. After the search for insights into who I really was, it became so important to discover my roots and the truth behind my family's secret. My father was born out of a love relationship during the Second World War. The secret that he was not the child of my Dutch grandfather had been hanging over our family for more than 60 years.

I chose to listen to my instincts and my heart to move forward, even though not everyone was happy about me going on this search. I respectfully asked my father if he would be okay with it and I got his approval, though this was after I had already booked the tickets to Italy.

Open to new adventures

While booking all the tickets and hotels for my trip to Italy, I happened to come across a lovely Italian man through an online dating website. According to his profile, he ticked all the boxes on my list, plus he was good looking.

He happened to be coming to the Netherlands, where I lived, the week before I was to travel to Italy so we decided to meet at the airport. When he came out of the gate I knew immediately that he was The One. As I watched him walk towards me, I saw images of us getting married, having children, and creating a wonderful life together. But I wasn't going to tell him that on our first date! He would have jumped right back on that plane (or at least that's what I thought).

We had the most amazing lunch and as thoughtful as he is, he had brought me a bracelet with little hearts on it. After our lunch, and with butterflies in my belly, I drove to work. But for that week my mind constantly wandered off, until it was time for me to pack my bags and leave for Italy.

He helped me unravel our family secret in 4 days and we fell madly in love. Four amazing days were all it took to feel that calm and peace in my heart, soul and being. We were let into old military archives in Modena, Italy and the municipality gave more information than they were actually allowed to give. I understood there and then that we were being helped in spirit by my biological paternal grandfather. Right before I travelled back to the Netherlands, I told my new man that I loved him and was anxious for his reply. Tears pooled in his eyes and he told me he loved me too. My heart jumped for joy. The man that I had been asking for had arrived.

I needed to be patient for a year, as we travelled back and forth between Milan and Groningen. During that year our longing for each other grew out of proportion. He asked me to marry him half a year into our relationship and we married a year later in the Netherlands, with all our beloved family and friends nearby. I wanted to have my dear grandmother present when we sealed our love — a love that perhaps would not have existed if she hadn't fallen in love with her Italian man.

I praise my grandmother every day for giving life to my father in brutal circumstances and for deciding to keep him when her family demanded she give him up for adoption right after she had given birth. And I praise her every day for her bravery and motherly instincts right after WWII as a single mum of 21 years young.

After our wedding, I moved to Italy. Leaving everything I'd ever known behind, I quit a well-paid management job, emptied my apartment and went — just like that — knowing in my heart it was the right step with the right man. Learning to trust my instincts in smaller instances helped me to trust them in bigger, life-changing ones like this. A month later we took a nice trip to visit Rome and 3 weeks after that we discovered I was pregnant. This baby was so welcome because I knew she would close my family's circle of shame and secrecy.

Much love,
Margaretha Tosi – Lesman
Milan

About the Author

Margaretha has reinvented her life completely after moving to Italy and becoming a mother. She is a Thought Leader, HypnoBirthing Practitioner, Magical Birth Keeper and a Spiritual Coach. She supports women and couples through pregnancy, birth and beyond. She lives near Milan, Italy and works globally to support future parents in this important phase of their lives. Being the bridge between 2 cultures and 2 or more languages she's always able to create balance during a life-changing phase in couples' lives.

Margaretha is a safe haven and very much in contact with our mother earth. She has a natural ability to create a safe space wherein you are allowed to release and let go of all (ancestral) hurt and pain so that you are able and willing to step into your full, powerful self — the person and parent that you are in the very core of your being.

She has a bold and much-needed vision for the near future to give families what they really need— a tribe and continuous care.

For HypnoBirthing visit www.hypnobirthingitalia.com or contact her via email margarethatosi@gmail.com

Conclusion

The stories in this book have probably opened your eyes to new possibilities. They certainly have done that for me. I hope that expanding your mind and exploring new ways to manifest love will bring you joy and fulfillment. Whatever way you decide to consciously co-create your soul-based relationship, please share it with us on our Facebook page: www.facebook.com/Share-Your-Story-with-Make-Your-Mark-Global.

I sincerely wish you an empowered journey to Conscious Love. If our paths should cross, I hope you will open up and share stories about your own experiences of manifesting love. You can send me an email so we can see proof of the magic this book inspires, or perhaps you'll do so in one of my upcoming books or a live event?

Feel free to contact the brilliant, brave authors in this book. They are so heart-centered and precious, I know they will inspire you as they have me. Besides, being in the company of amazing people allows their special sauce to rub off on us, and if we let it, their magical qualities can also linger.

Please visit YouTube to watch the #AskTheAuthor interview series and visit www.ManifestingLoveBook.com and sign up to receive special gifts from the authors.

Many blessings to you,
Andrea and all of the authors of *Manifesting Love*

Appendix

Find more resources from our authors by visiting www.ManifestingLoveBook.com

Below is a collection of books that have helped us prepare for and maintain conscious love relationships.

The Real Self Love Handbook by Andrea Pennington, MD

Getting the Love You Want by Harville Hendrix and Hellen LaKelly Hunt

Attached by Amir Levine and Rachel S. E. Heller

Attachment-focused EMDR by Laurel Parnell

Conscious Loving: The Journey to Co-Committment by Gay and Kathlyn Hendricks

Why Him, Why Her by Helen Fisher, PhD,

Mating in Captivity by Esther Perel

The Brain in Love by Daniel Amen, MD

We by Robert Johnson

About the Book's Creator

Dr. Andrea Pennington is an integrative physician, acupuncturist, meditation teacher, and international speaker who is on a mission to raise the level of consciousness and love on our planet. As a personal brand architect, media producer, and communications specialist, she leverages her 20+ years of experience in broadcast and digital media to proudly help healers, Light workers and coaches to bring their brilliance to the world through publishing and media production with Make Your Mark Global Media.

Dr. Andrea is also a bestselling author, international TEDx speaker and documentary filmmaker. For nearly two decades, she has shared her empowering insights on vitality and resilience on the *Oprah Winfrey Show*, the *Dr. Oz Show*, iTV *This Morning*, CNN, the *Today Show*, LUXE-TV, Thrive Global and HuffingtonPost and as a news anchor for Discovery Health Channel. She also produced a four-part documentary series and DVD entitled *Simple Steps to a Balanced Natural Pregnancy*.

Dr. Andrea has appeared in many print publications including *Essence, Ebony, Newsweek, The Sun, Red, Top Santé* and *Stylist*. She has also written or contributed to 13 books. She is the Founder of the #RealSelfLove Movement and hosts the *Conscious Love, Conscious Evolution* and *Conscious Branding* podcasts. As Founder of In8Vitality she blends her 'nerdy' mix of medical science, positive psychology, and mindfulness meditation to empower us all to show up authentically, love passionately, and live with vitality.

Visit Dr. Andrea online at:
AndreaPennington.com
RealSelf.Love
MakeYourMarkGlobal.com
In8Vitality.com

Get Social!
facebook.com/DrAndreaPennington
twitter.com/drandrea
linkedin.com/in/andreapennington
instagram.com/drandreapennington

Other Books Published by Make Your Mark Global

Holistic Healing
Created and Compiled by Andrea Pennington

The Top 10 Traits of Highly Resilient People
Created and Compiled by Andrea Pennington

The Real Self Love Handbook: A Proven 5-step Process to Liberate Your Authentic Self, Build Resilience and Live an Epic Life
by Andrea Pennington

The Ultimate Self-help Book: How to Be Happy, Confident & Stress Free, Change Your Life with Law of Attraction & Energy Healing
by Yvette Taylor

Magic and Miracles
Created and Compiled by Andrea Pennington

Life After Trauma
Created and Compiled by Andrea Pennington

The Magical Unfolding by Helen Rebello

The Orgasm Prescription for Women
by Andrea Pennington

Time to Rise
Created and Compiled by Andrea Pennington

The Book on Quantum Leaps for Leaders: The Practical Guide to Becoming a More Efficient and Effective Leader from the Inside Out
by Bitta. R. Wiese

About the Book's Creator

Turning Points
Compiled and Edited by Andrea Pennington

How to Liberate and Love Your Authentic Self
by Andrea Pennington

The Top 10 Traits of Highly Resilient People (Summary)
by Andrea Pennington

Daily Compassion Meditation: 21 Guided Meditations, Quotes and Images to Inspire Love, Joy and Peace
by Andrea Pennington

Eat to Live: Protect Your Body + Brain + Beauty with Food
by Andrea Pennington

MAKE YOUR MARK GLOBAL

Get Published
Share Your Message with the World

Make Your Mark Global is a branding, marketing and media agency based in the USA and French Riviera. We offer publishing, content development, and promotional services to heart-based, conscious authors who wish to have a lasting impact through the sharing and distribution of their transformative message. We also help authors build a strong online media presence and platform for greater visibility and provide speaker training.

If you'd like help writing, publishing, or promoting your book, or if you'd like to co-author a collaborative book, visit us online or call for a free consultation.

Visit www.MakeYourMarkGlobal.com

Call us at +1 (707) 776-6310 or

send an email to Andrea@MakeYourMarkGlobal.com

www.ingramcontent.com/pod-product-compliance
Lightning Source LLC
Chambersburg PA
CBHW070918080526
44589CB00013B/1344